BJ
2051
.S53
1989

Slawson, Judith.

The second wedding
handbook

$7.

BJ
2051
.S53
1989

Slawson, Judith.

The second wedding
handbook

$7.95 69 83459

DATE		
BORROWER'S NAME		
SEP 2 7 1989		

ALSO BY JUDITH SLAWSON

ROBERT DUVALL:
Hollywood Maverick

LEGAL AFFAIRS

The Second
WEDDING
Handbook

The Second WEDDING Handbook!

A Complete Guide to the Options

Judith Slawson

A DOLPHIN BOOK

DOUBLEDAY

New York London Toronto Sydney Auckland

Produced by Ultra Communications, Inc.

A DOLPHIN BOOK

Published by Doubleday, a division of Bantam Doubleday Dell Publishing Group, Inc. 666 Fifth Avenue, New York, New York 10103

DOLPHIN, DOUBLEDAY, and the portrayal of two dolphins are trademarks of Doubleday, a division of Bantam Doubleday Dell Publishing Group, Inc.

LIBRARY OF CONGRESS CATALOGING-IN-PUBLICATION DATA

Slawson, Judith.
    The second wedding handbook : a complete guide to the options / Judith Slawson. — 1st ed.
      p.   cm.
    "A Dolphin book."
    ISBN 0-385-24677-3 (pbk.) :
    1. Weddings—Handbooks, manuals, etc. 2. Remarriage—Handbooks, manuals, etc. I. Title.
BJ2051.S53 1989
395'.22—dc19
                                      88-24079
                                         CIP

Book design by Kathryn Parise

*For all those men and women with the
courage to take a second chance on marriage
and the wisdom to make it work.*

CONTENTS

~ Contents ~

∼ Contents ∼

INTRODUCTION

This One's for You

You've done what you never thought you would again—fallen in love and decided to marry—and now you face the planning of your second wedding. This is when you get hit with the déjà vu blues, that feeling that you've been here before and it ended badly—in a divorce—or sadly—in the death of your spouse, and here you are back to square one. It's enough to give you second thoughts about this whole second marriage. This is the time to make up your mind that your second wedding is going to get the new marriage off to a wonderful start, which is all yours—and his.

First of all, keep in mind that you are not alone. Each year more than 930,000 women in the United States marry for the second time, so you have plenty of company in the decisions with which you're now dealing. Like you, they are wrestling with the problems of how to make this second wedding a meaningful and joyful celebration, without doing a replay of the first one. The solution to this dilemma is contained in the following imperative to you and your fiancé—*suit yourselves!*

Remember, you're all grown up now, something you may well not have been the first time. First-time brides, even if they marry after several years of being on their own, tend to bring It all home to Mom—"It" being the exhaustive arrangements and zealous management of the wedding. But that's all behind you now. A highly confident woman with a sturdy control on the rudder of your life, you will take charge of this second wedding from the overall concept to the smallest detail.

A second wedding has the aura of one of those mythical second chances of which we all dream. This is your chance to get it right, meaning whatever works best for you. If your first wedding was all white lace and orange blossoms, a tradition-bound ceremony followed by a lavish reception, you will probably want a simpler ritual in a less formal mode. If, on the other hand, your first wedding was a skimpy affair and you've never stopped wishing it had been a more substantial event, now is the time to do it with all the frills.

No matter how thoroughly you go about either modifying or elaborating on your first wedding, your second one should not be a correction of that earlier experience. Rather, it is to be the expression of a woman who has learned enough from life to have the courage of her convictions. Your tastes are by now more sharply defined, your values more firmly established. That is why this book isn't full of do's and don'ts, or rules and proscriptions. You don't need a handbook to tell you what you are supposed to do. You need one to offer suggestions from which to pick and choose those which strike your fancy and fire your imagination. The only given to remember as you prepare for your second wedding is that there are no rules.

So brush off those déjà vu blues like insignificant crumbs at the table of your happiness. Take a good look at yourself and the man you are marrying. The two of you are a couple confident of your preferences in clothing, furniture, entertainment, and socializing. You have each refined your individual lifestyles and are combining them into a union which will be a vibrant personal statement. Your wedding should both reflect your separate styles and anticipate the united one on which you are embarking.

"The triumph of hope over experience" is how Samuel Johnson described a second marriage. Better to look upon the second marriage as a tribute to the ability to learn from experience. Make these second nuptials your distinctive way of saying that this marriage will be a meaningful and enduring union. Now you can joyfully celebrate the strength and depth of a love which inspires two separate human beings to blend into one wedded couple.

The Second
WEDDING
Handbook

CHAPTER ONE

Engagement Encore

Modest Proposals

Proposals, whether on bended knee or feet planted solidly on the floor, went out with the Victorian novel, but there is still that exciting moment when two people—with emotions ranging from trepidation to exultation—agree to share their future. This is one of the most precious experiences life has to offer, to be cherished as it happens and then enshrined in the couple's joint memory.

You can start setting an individualized tone for your second marriage by selecting the style of engagement which best suits you and your fiancé. The engagement period for a second marriage is usually more casual than for the first, which is rife with rituals such as diamond rings, newspaper announcements, and a lavish party thrown by the prospective bride's proud parents. Now you are free to browse among these traditions, retaining and discarding as you wish.

Whether your engagement is to stretch out over several months of planning an elaborate wedding, or is to be a two-week interval before a trip to City Hall, it remains a distinctive period with markings all its own. Make the most of it.

"I underplayed the engagement period of my second marriage," recalled Peggy, a vivacious account executive at a major West Coast advertising agency. "Because my first marriage ended in divorce, I thought it was in poor taste to make a big fuss over the decision to get into a second one. Now I regret that I didn't do more. Joy is joy and should be spread around whether or not the experience is a new one."

Private Pronouncements

You and your fiancé will want to convey your joyful decision to certain people before you go public with it: namely, your children from your former marriage. The problem is that children are not necessarily going to hear your news with unmitigated delight, so whether you tell your children alone or in your fiancé's presence will depend on the nature of his relationship with them.

"I knew the kids would have a lot of problems about my remarriage and there was no way I was going to subject the man I was marrying to their hostility at hearing our plans," said one divorced mother whose children hadn't spent a great deal of time with their future stepfather.

"Ralph and I had been living together for a year and a half before we decided to make it legal," explained Ginny, the youthful mother of four. "The kids were crazy about him, and when we told them our plans, they were as thrilled as we were."

The situation between your man and your children probably lies somewhere between these two scenarios, so you will want to give some thought to the pros and cons of having him around when you tell them. But whether you're on your own in divulging your plans or he's by your side, make the news of this second marriage as easy for your children to digest as you possibly can. The best way to do this is to decide beforehand exactly what role they will play in your wedding. Then you can firmly assure them that they won't be excluded from the festivities.

If the man you're marrying has children, the question arises as to whether or not you should be there when he informs them of your plans. You may not know his kids as well as he knows yours because they probably don't live with him as yours most likely do with you. If he says he wants you there when he tells them, talk it over and decide if that is really the best way to handle this delicate issue. Be sure to be protective of yourself. If you suspect resentment will surface when his offspring hear they're about to acquire a stepmother, you just might choose not to be confronted with their anger in the midst of your happiness. Another point to keep in mind is that if they have to stifle an expression of their disapproval out of politeness to you, the unspoken resentment will fester, only to bubble up again when and where you are least prepared to deal with it.

A word of caution if both of you are parents and you are considering telling both sets of future stepchildren at the same time. Before you start figuring out what restaurant you're going to take them to when you make the announcement, give some thought as to how your children and his feel about one another. Unless a lot of time and effort has already gone into cementing these complex relationships, you can be sure that your news will in no way be greeted with joyful exclamations about how with six you get eggroll, à la the Brady Bunch.

Besides children, parents, and siblings, there may be others who have a right to be in on the news before it's public knowledge. If you're a widow and have remained close to your in-laws, you will want to personally tell them this news about which they are sure to have mixed feelings. Make this intimate announcement an opportunity to reassure them that they are not being banished from your life because you are remarrying. But if you have not yet introduced your future husband to your late husband's family, don't do so at the time you tell them of your plans to marry. Combining the introduction with the announcement could prove an overload on your in-laws' emotions. If they have already met your fiancé, you may or may not want to have him present when you break the news. If they haven't met him, tell them yourself and say you want very much for them to meet him.

If your first marriage produced children and ended in divorce, your ex-husband needs to hear the news directly from you before he hears it from anyone else. There is no point in pretending this isn't his business because it so strongly affects the lives of his children. It is also likely to have implications for your financial arrangements with him. Impart your news in a fashion ranging from neutral to friendly depending on the present state of relations between you and your former husband. Don't use this announcement as an opportunity to re-hash the past, tempting as it may be to resurrect old resentments. A new marriage is not only a new beginning for you and your future husband. It can also be a step toward more mature, less emotionally charged encounters with your former husband. The style in which you tell him of your plans can go a long way toward setting the tone for this new phase of your relationship with your children's father.

Public Announcements

Now it's time to tell the world, but how? Most conventional books of etiquette suggest that a second-time bride not send an announcement of her engagement to the newspapers but wait for the wedding announcement to get into print. Your own announcement mailed to close-by and far-flung family and friends, colleagues, and acquaintances will be more than sufficient to make your private plans public. In keeping with your aura of independence, you may want the announcement to come directly from you rather than your parents. This missive can be in the form of an elaborate printed statement or photocopies of a handwritten letter. One woman used the graphics card in her personal computer to compose the following message from herself and her fiancé:

> *Marion Shelby and James Flynn are happy to announce plans to marry in April. Our feelings at this time can best be summed up by the words of our favorite poem.*

There followed several lushly Romantic verses in a dazzling variety of type sizes, shades, and styles, accompanied by a sketch of the engaged couple, arms entwined.

If you prefer announcing your engagement by phone rather than mail, go ahead and call everyone to tell them the big news. Again, the only rules for you and your fiancé to follow are the dictates of your own taste. However, while doing it your way, avoid hurting feelings. Should you opt for phone calls, be sure that your close friends who know each other are told within the same time period. No one likes to feel that they were an afterthought when glad tidings were announced.

Parents, Parties, and Presents

At some point you can expect questions from your parents, who may be puzzled as to what their role is to be in these second nuptials. If this issue wasn't raised by the announcement, it could come up over talk about an engagement party.

"The first time I got married, we eloped and my mother felt cheated of all the festivities, so when I became engaged to my second husband, she urged me to let her give us a big engagement party," recalled an executive in her late thirties. "But Jim and I lead lives so far removed from that kind of parental connection, that the notion of my parents giving us an engagement party seemed absurd. In the end, I had to have it out with my parents, and it wasn't an easy conversation."

Should you find yourself having a similar discussion, try to be both firm and kind. Let your parents know their participation in the events surrounding your second wedding is very important to you. But make it clear that they cannot expect to have the same level of involvement in these plans as they did at the time of your first marriage. You should also be prepared for a debate about the meeting of the two families.

"When I got married the first time, my parents entertained my fiancé's family at their home with a formal dinner party. They expected to do the same when I told them I was getting married again," said a second-time bride who just turned thirty and is marrying a man in his middle forties.

A repeat of that earlier dinner didn't sit right with the engaged couple, so the man took his widowed mother, his brother, and his sister-in-law out to dinner with his fiancée and her parents. Another woman, a middle-aged mother of teenaged children, didn't feel comfortable about *her* mother entertaining her future husband's large family in a small apartment. Instead, she had them all to dinner in her sprawling suburban home to sample her excellent cooking. There is no reason why your parents can't entertain his family, or host your engagement party if that's what the two of you wish. Just be sure you're doing what *you* want rather than conforming to a familial pattern which no longer pertains to you.

Perhaps you like the idea of a member of your family giving you an engagement party but your parents are no longer living or are too far away to make this possible. There is no reason why you can't have a favorite aunt or a cousin with whom you've always been close host the party. One widow, aware that her mother-in-law felt very threatened by her remarriage, had the good sense to ask that lady if she wanted to give the engagement party. An accomplished hostess with a large home, the mother-in-law was both touched and flattered by the request. The elegant party she threw the engaged couple went a long way toward establishing a positive new basis for the relationship between these two women.

If you are planning a very small wedding for close family members and only a handful of select friends, you may want to have a large, lavish engagement party and invite all the friends and relations who won't be attending the marriage ceremony. This is the only circumstance in which engagement presents are appropriate. Otherwise, these gifts belong to a former era of much longer betrothal periods. When many of the people coming to the engagement party won't be at the wedding, the invitation to the engagement party can serve as an announcement of the event itself, since just about everybody to whom you want to impart your news will be on the guest list.

Whether it's a big bash or a smallish get-together, you and your fiancé can choose to host the engagement party yourselves. Or you can let a friend or relative who wants to give the fete for you do so. But if you don't feel a party to celebrate your decision to marry is for you, there are other social settings in which you can let your friends share your joy and participate in your plans. A series of relaxing brunches or lively suppers could provide an enjoyable, low-key way to mix and mingle your friends with his. One woman for whom this style worked well was Doreen. A sociable young lady with a lot of women friends, she was marrying a man recently relocated to her city who didn't know too many people there.

"There was no way I could have had a formal party with only Ken and the one or two men friends he's had a chance to make here, and my legion of female friends," Doreen explained. "I did, though, want him to meet the people I care about." Doreen's solution was to invite one of her friends to brunch each Sunday throughout the winter before the wedding. "Each guest got a Bloody Mary, a vegetable omelette, and an introduction to the man I was going to marry," she recalled.

Jewels of the Heart

Diamonds are still a girl's best friend, even the second time around, according to Tiffany's, and a diamond engagement ring is most often a solitaire.

If you find a diamond ring too reminiscent of an earlier engagement, you can opt for another precious stone. Emeralds, rubies, and sapphires are excellent choices for a ring that connotes a special event and says something more than simply "I am engaged to be married." Combining these with other stones, such as diamonds or pearls, can make the ring truly distinctive and very much "you." And if size is important to you, you can have more of a "rock," since rubies and sapphires are less costly than diamonds.

One way to personalize your engagement ring is to select a stone which reflects a specific attribute of yours. This is what Princess Diana did when she chose a sapphire suggestive of her blue eyes. Sarah Ferguson followed suit by picking out a ruby to highlight her red hair. Give some thought to which stones might suggest something special about you. Another individualized touch which might make sense to you is to take your birthstone as the jewel to set in the ring signifying your engagement. Look through the following list of birthstones and see if the one representing the month of your birth appeals to you for this purpose:

January	garnet
February	amethyst
March	bloodstone
April	diamond
May	agate or emerald
June	agate or emerald
July	ruby or onyx
August	carnelian
September	chrysolite or sapphire
October	aquamarine or opal
November	topaz
December	ruby

Should an understated style appeal to you, semiprecious stones could be what's called for, as would any antique ring which catches your fancy. You could also take an older ring, perhaps a family heirloom or one you've had since childhood, and redesign it, adding more stones to create something totally new. It is probably not a good idea to do this with the engagement ring from your first marriage. Since you and your future second husband are making a fresh start, recycling a gem with such a complex personal history could cause subtle but significant problems. But if you want to keep the first ring, it can be made into another piece of jewelry, such as a circle pin or a pendant attached to a slender gold chain worn around the neck. The ring can also be embedded in a thick gold choker.

Even though you are probably planning to have a double-ring wedding ceremony, you can still use the engagement as an occasion to exchange rings with your future husband. A signet ring with his initials, a semiprecious stone such as peridot or beryl, or a specially designed one-of-a-kind ring would be good choices. Should your fiancé not be interested in wearing a ring, you can give him a special memento to celebrate the engagement.

Any number of stylish personal items would serve this purpose. Cuff links, a belt buckle, a case to carry business cards, a comb and brush set, monogrammed buttons for a special blazer, an elegant desk set for his office, or a money clip made out of silver or gold are all good possibilities for such a gift. One wife-to-be presented her fiancé with a small silver box for jewelry that had the first stanza of their favorite song engraved on the lid. You can also use the engagement present to start a collection, for example, of silver or gilded shot glasses, beautiful pieces of sculpture done in marble or crystal, or paintings by respected artists. This way, you can add to the collection with each anniversary.

Whether you throw a glittering party and wear a large square-cut diamond on your finger, or have a few friends over for a homey celebration with a simple garnet on your ring digit, your betrothal should be brimming with special moments. Don't let yourself get so bogged down with details and immersed in wedding arrangements that you forget to savor every second of the engagement period. Stay aware of just how precious and how fleeting is this sweet stretch of time between your private promises to each other and your public exchange of vows. Because you're so much more experienced now than when you were engaged for the first time, you know enough to squeeze every last drop of joy out of every happy moment.

CHAPTER TWO

Second-Time Showers

Two schools of thought prevail about showers for a second wedding. One is that, like lightning, they shouldn't strike twice, but belong in the once-in-a-lifetime category. The other viewpoint says, life is short and showers are sweet, so why not?

Since the latter adage best fits your outlook, you'll want to adopt it as your own. From here you have two options. You can play it passive as a traditional bride would, and hope that your friends have sufficiently psyched you out to know you want them to toss you an avalanche of gifts. The alternative is to take charge of the situation with varying degrees of initiative. If your circle of friends includes that one woman you just know is not going to let a wedding appear on the horizon without planning a shower, you might drop a hint to her about your preferences in the matter.

Well, what exactly are they? Certainly not a duplication of the shower you had well over a decade ago when you really needed those hand towels and place mats, were wildly grateful for an electric can opener, and felt ecstatic over a toaster oven. Nor do you necessarily want to swing the other way and be given a catered brunch by friends whose gifts are substantial enough for a wedding rather than a shower. The trick is to keep the original intent of the shower—a warm and simple gathering for the bestowal of small gifts—without doing an encore of a scenario which belongs to an earlier era of your life.

A good way to retain an informal tone and keep the presents appropriately inexpensive, without taking an awkward step backward to basics in the gifts department, is to have a thematic shower. Unlike those early days when you needed necessities, your current wishes can be better met by focusing on a particular interest or hobby. Thematic showers also allow you to throw your own rather than have a friend do it for you.

There is no reason why you can't host your own shower if you show some style and savvy in putting the event together. How? By calling it a "celebration of my upcoming marriage," or "a party in honor of my wedding." Worded with such flair, your invitation suggests an enjoyable and original occasion in which your friends will be eager to participate.

You might want to structure your theme around a new skill you are cultivating for this new marriage. If you're a bit weak in the culinary arts, but are wanting to learn more, perhaps a "Kitchen Know-how Party" would do the trick with the wording of the invitation something like: "This time around, I'm going to cook, too."

Maybe you are moving to a new apartment after your marriage and would appreciate gifts to fit the special color scheme you're following. Perhaps you prefer to be more flamboyant in your choice of themes. One woman who decided on a lingerie shower sent out invitations to a party with a mock newspaper headline that read "Sexy Career Girl Finally Lands Husband." The gifts were all sumptuous lingerie from specialty shops like Victoria's Secret and other boutiques featuring the most exquisite and exotic in boudoir attire.

Hosting your own shower is a good way to let your friends give to you while you provide a pleasant social occasion. Playing both gracious hostess and prospective bride probably suits your current active style better than the more passive part of squealing with delight and amazement as your friends greet you with cries of "Surprise!" Throwing your own shower is very much in keeping with the varied social life of the accomplished, experienced woman.

In youth one's friends tend to come from a cohesive group so that your first shower was probably a gathering of girl-friends most of whom knew one another well. Now that you have had time to acquire friends from disparate parts of your life such as graduate school, several jobs, and professional associations, it's less likely that most of them know each other. Therefore, it makes sense that the invitation come directly from you rather than from one "best friend."

This point, that you now have a more complicated social life than at the time of your first marriage, raises another interesting option for your second shower. Believe it or not, no law exists which says that only women can be invited to a shower. You just might not want your second one to be a strictly female affair. The possibility of including the man you are going to marry and his friends on the guest list is one you'll want seriously to consider. If you decide to take the plunge and break with tradition on this one, you could play it up for all it's worth with invitations beginning, "You are invited to a coed shower," or using a mock newspaper headline such as, "World's First Unisex Shower Debuts." Thematic showers can provide the perfect opportunity for including men on your guest list. It's a chance to do something different and span a bridge between the His and Hers categories of friends.

Take your clues for your theme from the things which intrigue you as a couple, which will be important in your shared future. Perhaps you and your lover are already sharing a weekend house. A "Back to Nature" party would prompt friends from both sides of the aisle to give you gadgets for the rural retreat. Presents purchased for a new sailboat, furnishings for a hunting/fishing cabin, or any kind of sports equipment, would all be well received.

Using your imagination, you'll be able to work the gift theme into your menu and decorations. For instance, if the gifts are centered around the sailboat on which you and your intended plan to spend a lot of time, you can have a nautical decor. A trip to a boating store will supply you with flags from various vessels to hang on the wall along with compasses and navigational maps. A few captain's chairs in your living room and some sailor suits for you and your fiancé might be just the right touch. Food can follow the gift and decor theme by serving a meal of homemade chowder, freshly caught fish, and sharp-tasting coleslaw. Beer is definitely the appropriate beverage for such a meal, which can be concluded with a cake in the shape of a sailboat.

There are distinct advantages to opening up the shower to include that half of the species which has never been included in this particular prenuptial ritual. For openers, it affords the opportunity of getting your friends and his together in an informal setting so that when they meet at the wedding it will seem like old home week. It's an easy, no-sweat way to mix and match social sets, and can be more appropriate to contemporary mores than the traditional ladies-only bridal shower.

Just as your women friends are more diverse now than at the time of your first marriage, the roster of those close to you is also likely to include a few men. There may be a male colleague at work with whom you are closer to than many of the women you would automatically invite. Your fiancé may also have close friends of the opposite sex. You're no longer living in the world where sorority sisters give the showers and frat brothers throw the bachelor party. Life is more varied, complex, and flexible these days, so a coed shower lets you include your favorite office crony who happens to be male and your fiancé's close business colleague who is female.

This way the shower can become a microcosm of the wedding you'll soon be planning because invitations will come from both of you, and prospective wedding guest lists can be merged. But unlike the roster for the wedding, a shower's guest list need have no imperatives such as relatives you're not all that close to, or work associates you may feel obligated to invite.

This shower should be a purely fun occasion for the genuine friends in your lives, and can ignore both familial and business obligations. Invite only those people you like and whom you feel would add to the merriment of the occasion. The wording of these invitations should convey the thematic nature of the event. Set the tone for an informal, lighthearted gathering in which expensive and ostentatious gifts would be out of place. If it's going to be coed and you choose not to use the word "shower" in the invitation, be sure you don't say "engagement party." That connotes a lavish affair and more extravagant gifts than you have in mind. Handwritten notes are what you need here. Their message should be that you want your most cherished friends to join in the launching of your official couplehood by showering you with tokens of the lifestyle you will be sharing:

A pair of swinging singles on the path to couch potatohood, Nancy Ryan and Jim Mallory invite you to brunch at noon on Sunday, May 24, to celebrate our engagement. Additions to our video cassette library most welcome. RSVP

Such an invitation shows how high-tech innovations can be inexpensive, fun-to-buy items. They also provide entertainment possibilities. You could, for instance, record the festivities on your VCR and play them back for the participants. Or if you're starting out your new life by replacing the *His* and *Hers* record albums with *Our* Compact Discs, let the CDs your guests bring be the background music for the gathering. In this circumstance, you'd better specify just which type of music you are collecting.

Inexpensive computer software or minor gadgets for the

shared photography hobby of the new couple are other possibilities for timely presents. Another way to have the gift theme express your specific styles and interests is for the occasion to assist each of you in acquiring a hobby of the other. Let your guests feel a part of the process by this type of invitation:

> Your help is requested to make a fisherwoman out of Kate and a horseman out of John. Whatever accoutrements can be acquired to this end will aid her efforts to become a flycaster par excellence and his attempts to look at home on a horse.

Gift suggestions will challenge the ingenuity of your friends and definitely break the ice in introducing the two social sets. Maybe you've been racking your brains for a subtle way to introduce your fiancé's fishing pal to the woman with whom you go horseback riding. What could provide a better opportunity than an easygoing atmosphere where they can each chat so pertinently about their sports enthusiasms? In an era where many marriages are second ones for both halves of the engaged couple, friends may feel awkward meeting the successor to the spouse of whom they have been fond. What better way to get past this social hurdle than having those friends shower the new couple with gifts which will be building blocks in cementing this second marriage?

Now that you've found your theme, made your guest list, and are eager to try your hand at writing a sprightly phrased invitation, you should pause to think through where this new-style shower is to take place. Circumstances count for much in these considerations. If you live way out in the suburbs, an invite to a barbecue on a summer Sunday afternoon is just fine. But asking people on a guest list of mostly city dwellers to make the trek on a winter Friday evening when the roads are likely to be slick with sleet and choked with traffic is another matter. Your fiancé's city apartment would be far more appropriate for the latter situation. But what if the apartment is a very small one and your list has swelled to about two-dozen people?

This is a situation in which you can combine the old-fashioned and newfangled shower styles into one convenient package. If you have a very close friend whom you suspect has been already planning a shower for you, take her into your confidence about your own plans and she'll probably be happy to have your party in her home. The invitations can still be from you or, if you like, from her. In this case, indicate that you are in on the arrangements and have expressed your preferences in the way of presents. You might offer to do the cooking for the gathering, or perhaps another friend who takes pleasure in turning out gourmet delights would like to volunteer. Maybe your fiancé, or his best friend, would like to prepare a brunch while you do the dessert. The possibilities are endless if you keep your mind in a flexible mode.

Remember, though, that being flexible doesn't mean jumping at each new suggestion if it's not for you—or him. If the man you're marrying can't handle the idea of including himself and his friends in the shower, don't press the point beyond a lively discussion. You are always free to shift gears and return to the "For Females Only" format. If that's to be the case, you might as well play it up by doing something gushingly feminine like a tea party replete with crustless watercress sandwiches or a frilly pink-and-white dessert like coconut cake and raspberry sherbet. On the other hand, you may be marrying a Texan, and whether or not he's present, you may want to show off your newly acquired abilities in Tex-Mex cooking with a chili supper or an eggs ranchero brunch.

But keep in mind that however scrumptious the food you serve, a shower is not quite like any other party. If you have created a theme around which your guests have purchased the presents, they will have put a lot of thought into their selection. Therefore, it behooves you to lavish as much energy on the receiving of these gifts as has been spent in picking them out. To give these tokens of affection their proper place, they should be opened in front of all the assembled guests at a carefully chosen time. Between the main part of the meal and the dessert and coffee to follow usually works well.

The second-time shower, like everything else about this second wedding of yours, is just that—yours. Let it express your tastes and give your friends a chance to do the same.

CHAPTER THREE

Setting the Date

March winds, April showers, May flowers, and June brides—
how neatly it all used to fit together. But our lives aren't so
neat these days—more exciting, yes, but usually so harried that
clearing the decks for a special occasion can take a good bit of
juggling on both the bride and the groom's part. Between the
demands of two careers and often two sets of kids, time for the
wedding must be carved out when it is most convenient for
many different schedules, which is not necessarily in the
month of June.

You'll find that if you stay flexible when selecting the date,
you may well help determine the style of your wedding and the
locale of your honeymoon.

Adrienne, a hospital dietician, whose briskly efficient manner belies her truly romantic imagination, wanted her second
wedding to be the dream experience her first one wasn't. The
first time around, Adrienne had eloped and her "honeymoon"
turned out to be one night in a dreary motel. Now she was
determined to do things differently. Since her fiancé had never
been married before, she wanted the occasion to be very special for him, too. But June was out of the question, conflicting

as it did with Jim's work schedule. A college administrator in charge of the summer school registration, he was busiest in June. Later in the summer conflicted with the work, travel, and study plans of the six children Adrienne and Jim had between them.

"A cold-weather wedding didn't feel right to me and spring was too long off, so we opted for autumn," Adrienne recalled. "We chose the Sunday of Columbus Day weekend because it's in the middle of what for most people is three days off and that made everything easier. Since we knew our guests wouldn't hit the usual Sunday night traffic driving home, we had the wedding at a country inn rather than in the middle of the city."

The beauty of the peaking fall foliage in so serene a setting lent a special splendor to the day which made it magic, as was the night they spent in the four-poster bed in the inn overlooking the woods.

The next morning, the newlyweds drove to the airport and were off on a two-week trip to Greece. The fares and hotel accommodations were at the off-season rates and the summer crowds were long gone, but gentle weather still lingered on those fabled islands. Instead of the bite in the air of a Northeastern autumn, the honeymooners enjoyed sunny days and evenings of soft winds.

It was Adrienne and Jim's practical choice of an October holiday weekend for their marriage which enabled them to choose a magnificently romantic setting for the ceremony and made the timing perfect for an idyllic and affordable honeymoon. Another couple, who chose a day not traditionally associated with weddings, deliberately picked an off-beat date which gave their marriage a unique feeling.

"The last thing I wanted was to be a June bride for the second time," said Eleanor, a research chemist with a flair for the exotic. Her first wedding when she was in graduate school was financed by her parents and completely in keeping with tradition, including the June date. The mother of two teenagers, Eleanor was in her early forties when she married Bill, a widowed father of four. The engaged couple sat down with a calendar and all six of their offspring to select a feasible day for the wedding festivities.

"How about Halloween so I can be a witch and flower girl at the same time?" Bill's eight-year-old daughter suggested.

"After carefully explaining to Jennie that witches don't walk down aisles strewing roses, Bill and I realized that she might have hit on something. We liked the idea of picking a day with something special about it," Eleanor remembered.

"Valentine's Day seemed too corny for a pair of middle-aged parents and the Fourth of July too complicated to fit into summer vacation schedules, so we kept racking our brains and poring over the dates till my oldest daughter came up with a winner—Groundhog Day, which fell on a Sunday that year."

It was perfect, Eleanor and Bill decided. February 2, the time of year when dead of winter softens into late winter, a harbinger of spring whether or not the groundhog sees his shadow. People are coming out of January's post-holiday gloom, and are ready for a party. Yes, Groundhog Day it would be, they all decided with a unanimous vote.

Selecting so whimsical a date for the wedding turned out to be the determining factor in its style. Eleanor's closest friends were charmed with the idea. One who had just started a cottage-industry greeting card business volunteered to make invitations with a sketch of a sleepy groundhog staring into the rays of a rakishly winking sun. Another friend, a free-lance writer, who had moved out of the city to a charmingly restored country barn, offered his barn for the wedding because the location fitted the date's significance.

The tone of the invitation, plus the rural setting, brought out an old-fashioned spirit in many of Eleanor's friends who, although they lived contemporary lifestyles, yearned for the mores of a simpler time. The wedding feast was a buffet, with each friend supplying a different dish, and dessert was a chocolate mousse molded into the shape of a groundhog.

Best of all, their simple country wedding left the newlyweds with more money for the honeymoon than they had expected.

"At first when we chose a winter date, we planned a ski trip," Eleanor said, "but all along I had a nagging feeling that wasn't what I really wanted. Because Bill and I live in Boston and often go skiing in Vermont, that sounded like fun but it didn't seem special enough, or as romantic as a honeymoon should be.

"Actually, this reservation about the honeymoon was in the back of both our minds. Neither of us wanted to bring it up to the other, however, because money wasn't exactly a nonissue for us. With the kids to raise, and our plans to buy a house larger than our separate homes, we were counting every penny. That's why when the groundhog idea snowballed and made our wedding so much simpler and less expensive than we'd planned, leaving us with a nice chunk of money, we changed our honeymoon plans."

The evening of their wedding found Eleanor and Bill on a plane bound for South America, where it was summer and the setting as much a novelty for them as they could ever hope to find.

For these two couples, the day before Columbus Day and the day of the groundhog's emergence were choices which had serendipitous results. But for other prospective brides and grooms, a particular day is at the core of their wedding plans from the start. Donna and Ralph were such a couple.

"The truth is that I was already pregnant when I got married the first time," said Donna, a winsome, thirty-seven-year-old brunette. Donna was savoring some well-earned happiness since her engagement to a colleague at the brokerage house where she worked as an investment counselor.

"Neither my first husband nor I really wanted to get married, but we both felt trapped into it. The ceremony at City Hall took five minutes, and there were far too many resentments on both sides for a romantic mood," Donna said in a tone of wistful regret.

"After the marriage ended, I had some rough years and swore I'd never marry again, but then I met Ralph and I knew it could work with us. I'm determined that this marriage will be different, starting with the wedding. I want the most romantic wedding imaginable," she explained.

What day spells romance? Donna asked herself as she and Ralph discussed their second wedding. The answer was surprisingly simple—Valentine's Day. Donna took care of all the details herself, and began making plans months in advance.

"We're both well into our thirties, so I don't want anything that looks like a teenaged prom in a gym with crepe-paper hearts," she said, laughing. After doing some research into the romantic fetes of more flamboyant eras, Donna decided that a masked ball such as was popular in eighteenth-century Venice would suit her craving for the lushly romantic. She rented the banquet hall of an elegant hotel and designed the invitation, which told the guests to come in costume and, of course, masks.

Donna wore a period ivory satin dress with tight bodice and stiff skirt. She carried a mask in the same shade and material as her dress, mounted on the end of an exquisitely carved handle. The ceremony took place by candlelight and then the ball commenced, replete with an orchestra whose specialty was the Viennese waltzes popular at the Venetian court. An extravaganza in every sense of the word, Donna noted cheerfully. It was her second chance to have the wedding of her dreams, with a dazzling sheen of baroque opulence.

The way Donna felt about Valentine's Day was the way Marie thought of Mardi Gras. Raised in New Orleans where Mardi Gras is the highlight of a flamboyant week of winter carnival, Marie wanted to recapture that magical atmosphere from her childhood on the day of her marriage. Although Marie's second wedding took place in San Francisco, where her fiancé and all their friends lived, the celebration was an exuberant Mardi Gras party, which for Marie will always symbolize a day of joy.

Equally romantic in their choice of a wedding day were Lorraine and Phil, a pair of computer programmers whose fanciful choice of a wedding date belied their ultrapractical profession. They became engaged in the month of October, and they decided they wanted the wedding to take place at the end of the following winter, which happened to be a leap year. Since the end of February worked out well for their office schedules, they selected the twenty-ninth of that month for their wedding. Why pick a day that only comes once every four years? The question, of course, was one they heard frequently and for which they had a ready answer.

"First of all, the day had a particular significance to us because it was Lorraine who actually raised the marriage issue," said Phil. His two previous marriages had ended unhappily, and he didn't have the nerve to initiate the commitment for a third. "The day she proposed wasn't even in leap year but since the twenty-ninth of February is associated with the woman popping the question, the day symbolized Lorraine's great emotional courage in taking a chance on us," Phil explained.

"And we figured that since we would only have an anniversary every four years, we would make each one the occasion for a truly extravagant vacation," Lorraine piped in. The couple also had great fun writing the wedding invitations, which included a clever paragraph about the origins and rationale of Leap Year Day in the calendar every four years, as well as a witty little ditty about Sadie Hawkins.

Couples who are original in their choice of a wedding date often become very creative when planning invitations and decorations. Some brides and grooms who selected the day on which they met to get married include a few lines about their meeting in the invitation. Two people whose first encounter was at a dude ranch used a Western-style motif for their wedding and had a barbecue in the bride's Pennsylvania suburban home. Another couple, who celebrated their wedding on the first anniversary of their meeting on a cruise ship, recreated the scene at a local waterside restaurant.

Other couples select their wedding date with an eye to familial conveniences. "We wanted to include all of Jack's far-flung family, as well as mine, who happen to live closer to us, so we got married over the Labor Day weekend, which is the time his whole family gets together for a gigantic picnic," said Nancy. "Of course, we didn't have the wedding at the picnic," she hastened to explain, "but it was the only way of making sure that Jack's whole family could be present."

For Joanne, the Fourth of July bash which her close circle of friends have at a lake every summer was the perfect time—and place—for her nuptials. For Lois, it was her sister's Thanksgiving dinner for the family, which was expanded to include the wedding celebration. Margaret, too, took advantage of a family Thanksgiving gathering to have her wedding, but she held the ceremony on the Saturday of the four-day weekend. Another couple whose children attended different colleges around the country combined their wedding with a New Year's Day celebration marking the end of the children's school vacation period, when all the offspring were home.

Such practical considerations in setting the date are not to be scoffed at, given the strains on the schedules of contemporary couples. But keep in mind that it is *your* wedding and the accommodations you make to others' timetables should only be those with which you both are entirely comfortable. In an effort to deal with time constraints two-career couples are often bound by, it's easy to forget the "suit yourselves" dictum, which is the basis of this book. But this is just the time when it should be kept most firmly in mind.

Remember, this is your wedding to *enjoy*, and not an exercise in running yourself ragged. If, when the two of you sit down with the calendar, your feeling is one of sheer panic— How am I ever going to get it all done?—then it's time to take another look at your options.

Like many people marrying for the second time, you may

find that it's impossible to take a large enough chunk of time off from your job to prepare for a wedding and for a honeymoon immediately following the wedding.

"I simply had to have the week preceding the wedding off," said Sally, a sales manager with a hectic work schedule. "This was my *wedding*, not a sales meeting, and I wanted to do it right with lots of time for the beauty parlor, luncheons with special friends, and time for the million last-minute details that have to be taken care of—not to mention time to soak in a bubble bath, and think about being the bride of the man I adore.

"So what I did," Sally continued, "was to establish priorities. I decided that the pre-wedding week came first, and that Tim and I could put off the honeymoon in Italy for another few months. That way Tim was able to take off the last two days of the week, and we made a marvelous four days of it, culminating with our Sunday wedding and brunch. True, it was back to work on Monday morning, but we still had the honeymoon to look forward to and we were both relieved to have some of the pressure taken off."

Setting your priorities is extremely important in the initial planning stages of the second wedding. If a particular date for the nuptials means a lot to you, you may have to accommodate your honeymoon plans to it, or separate the two events by a few weeks, or even months.

"I know this isn't romantic," a cooking school owner named Laurie said a bit sheepishly, "but Don and I wanted to be married right after we applied for a mortgage on the house we were buying. That was in late September. We had also long dreamed of a Caribbean honeymoon during the worst of winter when the contrasts between the warmth of the tropics and the interminable snow of an Albany January would be greatest."

Laurie and Don solved their problem with a wedding in early October, followed by a long Indian summer weekend at a delightful Victorian inn on the Jersey shore. Then in January, just after the closing on the new house, they took off for Aruba. Another couple, whose accountant strongly advised making their living arrangement legal by the end of the calendar year for tax purposes, had their wedding early in December and then took the April-in-Paris honeymoon they'd always dreamed of.

Not only can the honeymoon and the wedding be separated in time, so, too, can the ceremony and the reception. If, for some reason, you want the wedding to take place by a certain date, and it's not possible for everyone you want to invite to make it then, you can have a very small ceremony and hold the reception at your leisure when the time is better for your guests.

If separating aspects of your wedding doesn't suit you, don't even consider it. Just decide what is most important and build around that. One couple who had long planned on an Easter-in-Seville honeymoon fitted their wedding around it, although their children's separate spring vacation schedules caused some logistical problems. Another couple wanted to be married at an exclusive private home rented out for weddings, and took the first available date, although it meant changing their honeymoon plans accordingly. Then there was the couple to whom it was very important to be married by a particular priest who was soon going abroad on missionary work. The wedding reception and honeymoon plans were adjusted to fit the priest's schedule.

In selecting the date of your second wedding, the only rule to remember is to pick the one which feels right to both of you given the various constrictions and necessities for compromise in your very full lives. Just remember—*you* are selecting the date, the date is not selecting you, so pick the one with which you feel most comfortable and take it from there.

CHAPTER FOUR

Money Matters

Money *does* matter. Unless you're one of the fortunate few for whom it is no consideration, financial realities necessitate choices. The choices you make have much to say about the values by which you live and the styles with which you are most comfortable. Fiscal independence is an inherent part of taking control of your own wedding. Unless you and your fiancé are willing to relinquish a significant portion of that control, you have to be prepared to foot the bill for your own nuptials.

These days, even when a couple is marrying for the first time, the tradition of the bride's family paying all the costs of the wedding is giving way to more practical financial arrangements, especially with today's escalating costs. For a second wedding, it is rare that the bride's parents pay the entire bill. Usually the bride and groom pay for most, if not all, of the expenses themselves.

However, whether out of necessity or out of generosity, one or both sets of parents may want to pay for a particular portion of the wedding. Before you and your fiancé accept any of these offers, talk it over between the two of you so that you present a united front when dealing with well-meaning but sometimes inadvertently intrusive future in-laws.

The best way to handle this delicate situation is to accept only clearly defined and definitely limited gifts. Unless you want to make your mother an integral part of all the plans, it may not be a good idea to let her give the reception. But suggest that your parents take care of certain aspects of the reception such as champagne costs, or flower arrangements.

In the same but subtler vein, if your fiancé's parents offer to give you the honeymoon, you may not want to accept so magnanimous a gift but would be willing to have them give you the plane tickets for your wedding trip. In this way, you are graciously accepting generous parental offers, but making it clear that the two of you are assuming the major responsibility for every aspect of the wedding.

Even when the two of you decide to assume the entire financial burden, there are decisions to be made. For instance, is this burden to be assumed equally? If you're both investment bankers—no problem. But what if one of you is a highly paid attorney and the other a schoolteacher? One such couple had the additional complication of the woman being the higher earner.

"Jane and I hadn't had a problem with our income disparities when we were dating," explained Ted, an idealistic science teacher in an inner-city school, strapped with hefty child support payments from his first marriage.

"I think of myself as a contemporary kind of guy, your basic liberated male, but the idea of a woman picking up my tab goes against my grain, so Janey and I limited our activities to those which were within my means, provided we went dutch," Ted added with a good-natured grin.

Ted assumed that their wedding would follow the same egalitarian lines of their dating life, but he ran headlong into Jane's dreams. Her first wedding took place when she was struggling through law school. Jane's parents were always plagued with money problems, so she didn't think it fair to expect them to finance her wedding to a fellow law school student. A high achiever, Jane found it difficult to put aside her dream wedding for an affordable one the first time, and she refused to do so the second time around when the fashionable festivities she wanted were well within her means. Jane was more than willing to finance her second wedding in the style to which she felt her years of hard work had entitled her. Ted wasn't so sure he wanted a wedding paid for by the bride.

A tense period of discussion and compromise ensued, which prefigured many of the decisions this couple would face when they set up housekeeping together. What finally saved them was reverting to an old-fashioned layout of expenditures with a new twist. Jane footed the bill for what the bride's family traditionally pays for: the invitations and announcements, the ceremony, reception, and bridal gown. Ted took on the expenses once divided between the groom and his family, such as the bride's ring, marriage license, bridal bouquet, and clergy fee. The couple split the cost of the honeymoon, and everyone was happy.

Money matters very much when planning a wedding because, as Jane and Ted soon realized, the questions it raises can predict the pattern in which finances will be handled in the marriage itself.

Even if you and your future second husband have been living together for a few years, you probably have kept your finances separate, sharing rent and other common expenses but maintaining separate checking and savings accounts, not to mention long-term investments. In fact, many live-in couples who do take the matrimonial plunge find that combining finances is the biggest change in their lives.

"I think the financial aspects are what most confounded us when Frank and I sat down to discuss our wedding. We had been sharing an apartment for three years, renting a summer place together, and splitting the expenses on several vacations. So what was the problem about talking over wedding expenses?" Vicki asked herself. A pediatrician marrying a CPA,

Vicki wasn't worried about the money to be spent on the lavish wedding she and Frank were planning, but the topic raised other issues that were difficult for her to confront.

"My first marriage was a mess from a financial point of view, because my husband was an irresponsible spendthrift who put us both into debt. I vowed I'd never put my money at anyone's disposal again, but now that Frank and I were getting married, I knew I'd be dealing with joint tax returns, savings plans, and investment portfolios, and the idea terrified me."

When Vicki and Frank opened a joint checking account for the purpose of paying for the wedding, it was her first experience with this aspect of the marital commitment. In this way the wedding became Vicki's trial run for the adjustments her marriage would necessitate.

In a society where money is the means to status, it often has a symbolic value in human relationships. For men, making more money than women has always been tied in with issues of power and control. For women, earning as much money as a man is often the key to self-respect in personal as well as business matters. Power struggles are, unfortunately, all too often the stuff of interpersonal relationships. Money is often the ostensible issue in quarrels between men and women while the hidden problems of emotional hurt and sexual dissatisfaction are never discussed. If you and your fiancé are fighting about money, you would be well advised to take a look at what other discords these disputes might be masking.

People who have been previously married come to a second marriage with a cumbersome baggage of personal history, which can get in the way if they're not on guard against it. If a man's first wife spent his money carelessly, he may be tight-fisted about wedding plans, puzzling a fiancée who is used to his wining and dining her with abandon.

Talking about finances in the context of getting married can trigger old responses to certain situations in the new relationship. A woman who, as a first wife, didn't work outside the home and had to account to her husband for every penny she spent may chafe at her fiancé's questioning certain expenses related to the wedding. If she's been supporting herself since the end of her first marriage, she can misinterpret such questions as criticism and feel her hard-won independence threatened. In these situations, a lot of patience and understanding on the part of the couple is called for, but the rewards in a richer, deeper appreciation of the other's point of view will be well worth the effort.

The assumption that people who are more established in their lives have more money to spend on weddings than those just starting out may be true in dollars and cents, but not necessarily in available funds. Since most first weddings are usually parentally financed, a penniless young couple may have more nuptial funds at their disposal than their more mature counterparts with children to support, mortgage payments to meet, and the full burden of maintaining a middle-class lifestyle in an inflationary era. Unless you and your fiancé make enough money between you to rise above these considerations, you will have some budgeting to do when it comes to the wedding.

First, you'll want to make certain that your thinking about these priorities is similar if not identical. Sometimes in the first flush of engagement bliss, a man and woman will be too ready to agree to what their partner wants without hashing out their differences first. This premature accommodation can lead to resentments later on, so it's better for each of you to know where the other stands from the start. Also, men are used to taking a backseat to women when it comes to wedding plans. While this is not the attitude you want for the launching of your second wedding, you should be aware of the reality that your groom may be so conditioned. You, on the other hand, may go along with your man's priorities whether they are authentically yours or not.

To avoid such misunderstandings with their unfortunate potential for future grievances, try this revealing exercise. Study the list of ten wedding features given below. Then rank each of them, numbering them from 1 to 10 in order of importance to you. Give the list to your fiancé and ask him to do the same exercise without looking at your responses.

WEDDING FEATURES

(Ranked In Order of Importance)

Inviting all the family and friends we wish

Holding the reception outside the home

Having a sit-down dinner at the reception

Providing a full bar at the reception

Having an orchestra at the reception

Hiring a professional photographer to take wedding pictures

Having lavish floral arrangements at the ceremony and reception

Throwing an elaborate wedding rehearsal dinner

Providing accommodations for out-of-town family and friends

Having the honeymoon of our choice regardless of expense

Now study your beloved's priorities as compared with your own. This should make for some lively discussion. It should also help in the fine art of compromise, probably the most essential ingredient for the success of your second marriage. See where you can cut and paste the two lists so that they are more in accord.

At this point, you might want to take another look at your list and ask yourself the following questions:

1. Is this something I really want, or just think I should have?

2. Do I want this in the here and now or to make up for what I once missed out on?

3. Why is this particular item so important to me?

4. Is there any substitute for this item which would suit me just as well?

As you study your answers to these questions, the two of you can do some thinking about where you can cut corners without sacrificing that which is most important to each of you. Before deciding that the cost of a honeymoon will rule out a formal reception, read the last chapter of this book. A honeymoon does *not* have to be expensive to be exotic. And when you're budgeting the reception, remember that serving breakfast or brunch costs less than a luncheon or cocktail buffet, which, in turn, are less expensive than a formal dinner. If you're planning to be married in a church or synagogue which has facilities for a reception, it may be less expensive as well as more convenient to have both the ceremony and reception at the same location.

Beware of making false assumptions when trying to trim the fat off the wedding festivities. Unless you're planning a very small wedding with a lot of help from family and friends in food preparation, an at-home reception can cost much more than anticipated. Hiring a caterer not only is a big expense in your own home, but can also cost more than having the meal prepared by a hotel or restaurant. But don't forget that at the latter establishments, you have no control over the amount of liquor consumed. Contrary to popular belief, a buffet can cost more than a sit-down meal because more food is served over a longer period of time. But a buffet is likely to be more economical than a sit-down dinner which offers a choice of entrées. When price shopping, make sure hotels, caterers, and restaurants are quoting the full cost, including drinks, and that there are no hidden expenses such as sales taxes and gratuities.

Think about how you can utilize the network of friends and relatives in both your lives to lessen some of the financial burden. Someone close to you may be either a professional photographer or such a good amateur one that the difference is negligible for your purposes. If such a person is asking what you want for a wedding gift, perhaps you can suggest they give you their talent for your wedding album. The same may apply to a friend or relative who has a band. The musicians may not be professional but they may still be good, particularly if they play the kind of music you both enjoy. The same thing may be true of a friend who's a terrific cook and is getting up the courage to start her own catering business. If you accept her catered dinner as a wedding present, it may give her the impetus to start her own business.

Your previous wedding will, in many ways, influence the decisions you make about your upcoming wedding. If your fiancé has never been married, he may want a more formal wedding than you do. But if he was married before at a wedding which was a lavish event engineered by his first wife's family, he may now opt for the simplest arrangements. If your first wedding was a low-budget affair, you may want now what you missed out on then. This is definitely the time to cultivate the crucial skill of compromise.

As you both take a long, hard look at where expenses can be cut and compromises worked out, you'll find yourselves feeling closer to each other, more trusting. In fact, even if you and your fiancé are sufficiently affluent that money really isn't an issue, you may still want to draw up your own rating sheet and then compare results. The differences may surprise you. Questions of values, style, and personal needs play a big role in planning a wedding. Clashes in personal needs are often the crux of marital discord, so now is the time to begin tackling them.

CHAPTER FIVE

Religious Issues

If you and your fiancé are both of the same religion, you are likely to want a clergyman of your faith to officiate. But like everything else about second weddings, such a choice is not to be taken for granted. Richard and Alison were both raised in the Presbyterian Church, but neither had practiced their religion for a number of years. The former head of the law firm for which they both worked and where they met had become a judge. It was this man, a father figure to both of them, whom they turned to when looking for someone to marry them. In a similar instance, a pair of lapsed Lutherans living in a small town felt it would be more appropriate to be married by the elderly justice of the peace, who was a close friend, than the local Lutheran minister, with whom they had had very little contact.

The question of whether to be married in a religious or civil ceremony goes to the heart of basic values and philosophies of life. It is an issue which every couple will want to consider quietly, calmly, and thoughtfully before relating their thoughts to family and friends. Whatever the decision is, each of you should feel satisfied with it. If there are clashes in points of view, it is important to resolve them now.

Even when two people of the same faith want to be married by a clergyman, they may not desire a church wedding. "Roger and I are both Episcopalians who were each married previously in church ceremonies, but both our first marriages ended in divorce," explained Marjorie, a member of a socially prominent New York family. "We wanted our new marriage to be sanctified in the eyes of God, but the idea of a second church wedding didn't feel right to us." She and Roger were married in the spacious drawing room of her grandmother's town house with an Episcopal priest performing the elaborate and solemn ceremony. This was a compromise with which both bride and groom felt comfortable.

Maryann's experience with a church wedding was the opposite of Marjorie's. Raised in the Catholic faith, she left the Church while in college, and her first marriage, to a non-Catholic, was in a civil ceremony. Since the Church doesn't recognize the validity of such a marriage, Maryann was free to marry in the Church the second time, although her first marriage had ended in divorce. The man she was marrying was a practicing Catholic for whom this wedding would be the first.

"I felt as though I was coming home when my fiancé and I went to talk to the priest in his study," Maryann glowingly recalled. "We had a formal Mass, and I wore a white dress with my mother's wedding veil because as far as the family was concerned, this was my first wedding." Maryann's sense that this marriage was getting off to the right start was greatly enhanced because it was embedded in the tradition in which she was raised.

Similar sentiments were expressed by Norma and Sam, both Jewish, both marrying for the second time. Norma's first husband was also Jewish, but their wedding wasn't a Jewish one. "I got married in the early seventies in what is now known as a sixties wedding," Norma fondly reminisced. "We were both intensely involved in the peace movement and had a Quaker ceremony followed by a big party on the beach in Venice, California." Sam's first marriage was to a woman who was raised in the Catholic Church. Since neither Sam nor his first wife was interested in the possibility of one's converting to the other's faith, they were married by a Unitarian minister because "it seemed a sensible compromise," Sam explained.

Since both Norma and Sam had become more involved with Judaism in the last few years, they wanted their wedding to reflect their new religious commitment as well as the one they were making to each other. The wedding was held in a Reform temple they both attend. Another Jewish couple, Paul and Sandy, wanted to be married by a rabbi, but since neither had any affiliations with a synagogue in the city to which they had recently moved, they preferred to have the ceremony at the private club to which they both belonged and where they had met.

"The club was meaningful to us in a way that a synagogue wouldn't have been," Sandy said. "But we definitely did have a traditional Jewish wedding with a chuppa [wedding canopy] and, of course, Paul stamped on a glass to conclude the ceremony and all the guests cried out 'Mazel Tov.'"

If interfaith unions are proliferating for first marriages in our highly mobile, pluralistic society, they are even more prevalent in second marriages. Out in the work world with a social life based more on common interests than family background, the chances of falling in love with someone of a different faith are more likely. Although more second marriages happen between people of different religions than first ones, conversions to one spouse's particular faith are more common in first marriages. There are two reasons for this disparity: Parental wishes are more seriously considered in a first marriage, and a person's adult life patterns are more solidified in a second marriage.

"I converted to Judaism to please my first husband's parents," said Protestant-born Nancy. "My second husband was raised in the Catholic faith and continues to practice it, though not very consistently. His parents, particularly his mother, are very religious and urged me to convert to Catholicism. But I decided that one conversion to please in-laws per lifetime is quite enough," Nancy said tartly.

Another woman marrying for the second time also declined conversion to her fiancé's Jewish faith. Neither Carolyn nor her first husband, a Protestant like herself, practiced their faith, and their children were growing up without formal religious training. "If I were marrying for the first time, I could see myself converting," Carolyn said thoughtfully. "When I was younger, I was more malleable, less set in my ways, more open to taking on new identities. But now I'm more distinctly who I am, and it would go against my grain to do something which didn't really come from inside me."

Another woman, with a similar religious background and personal history to Carolyn's, did decide to convert to her husband's Jewish faith. But it wasn't simply a choice Sally made on her own. Rather than her own or her fiancé's parents playing a role in her decision, it was her children with whom she had to confer.

"Judaism is a faith with a central focus on religious practices in the home," explained Sally. "There was no way David and I could maintain a Jewish home which would include celebrating the Sabbath and all the holidays unless my children would be a part of it. Otherwise my conversion would end up being a divisive rather than a unifying factor in our family life." Sally's children, both in their preteens, were receptive to her conversion and their own instruction in their mother's new faith.

"It wasn't such a problem for them because they really had no religious identification of their own, as neither their father nor I were practicing Protestants. But had they already had religious training, or had their father objected to their being raised in their new stepfather's faith, I doubt that I would have converted to Judaism," Sally declared. Her qualifications shed some light on the complexities of this issue.

Sally did convert to Conservative Judaism and was married in a synagogue. She said that although her primary motivation in the conversion was to be able to share with her husband the rituals which meant a great deal to him, she wouldn't have done so unless the act was meaningful to her. "I don't think at this point in my life that I could take on a religion if doing so didn't fill a subjective spiritual need in myself," she said reflectively.

This attitude is typical of the woman entering a second marriage with a strong sense of self, with her identity firmly established. Most people marrying for the second time respect each other's differences, so there is less of a tendency for one to embrace the other's faith. There is often, however, the desire to add a religious dimension to the wedding ceremony itself, even if the couple is of different faiths and a conversion is not their choice.

The Reformed branch of the Jewish religion does have rabbis who will perform interfaith marriages, but finding one is up to the individual couple. When it comes to Conservative and Orthodox Judaism, interfaith marriages cannot be performed, and a Jewish person who has a civil divorce from a previous marriage must obtain a Jewish one. With Protestant denominations there is no fixed rule about interfaith marriages. It depends on the judgment of the individual minister performing the ceremony, who may feel, following pertinent counseling, that such a marriage is appropriate.

The Catholic Church allows for the marriage of interfaith couples provided a dispensation is granted by the chancery office of the local diocese. The interfaith couple is expected to participate in the same counseling sessions as are couples who are both of the Catholic faith. The Catholic party of the couple must sign a document promising that an attempt will be made to raise in the Church any children the marriage produces, but the non-Catholic party is no longer asked to make such a commitment. Should a Catholic whose first marriage took place in the Church and ended in a civil divorce wish to marry for a second time in the Church, an annulment of the earlier marriage must first be granted by the Church. A Catholic whose first marriage was not in the Church and ended in a civil divorce can marry in the Church, as the Church does not recognize the first marriage.

An interfaith couple considering a religious ceremony might want to have it performed by a minister of the Unitarian Church. Belonging to a highly liberal, flexible, and humanistic denomination, Unitarian ministers are willing to marry interfaith couples even if neither is a Unitarian. This would be a way to put the wedding ceremony into a spiritual context without a conversion or running into some of the problems interfaith couples face.

Like everything else about a second marriage, the question of a religious ceremony is very much up to the individual couple. If a conversion by one to the other's faith would be spiritually significant and emotionally meaningful, the couple should seriously consider this option. Since in most cases a conversion is not required for a marriage ceremony to be performed, religious ceremonies for interfaith couples are most often possible. These present a viable alternative both to conversions and civil ceremonies. In Chapter 16, "Standing on Ceremony," suggestions are given for adding a spiritual dimension to a civil ceremony. There is also a discussion on how to alter a standard religious ceremony to individual thoughts and feelings about marriage.

CHAPTER SIX

Selecting the Setting

Now that the when is settled, you'll want to turn your thoughts to the where. Generally, the sites of second weddings are more imaginative and less traditional than those of the first. Age and experience lend a hand to convention-shedding behavior. You trust your own impulses more and often give in to your own fantasies and ideas about romance. Having thrashed out your priorities with your fiancé and established a working budget, it's time to select the setting which best fits your dreams—and your finances.

The following wedding experiences should stimulate your thinking on the subject of just where to have this special occasion.

Romantic, Elegant, and Flamboyant

"Elegant flamboyance" describes Felicia's personal style, and that style was reflected in her second wedding. Meeting for a drink at a trendy midtown Manhattan club, where she is a member, Felicia was dressed on the cutting edge of fashion in a designer original green-and-blue patterned silk dress, her blond-streaked hair cut in a carefully casual style. The owner of a successful advertising agency, Felicia is in her midforties, very much her own woman—and very much in love with her second husband of less than a year, Nicholas.

"My first wedding was your basic father-financed traditional shindig. Unfortunately, the marriage which followed was a total flop. I was on my own for many years, making money, meeting men, learning a lot about life and a little about love. Then I met Nicholas and I knew what the lyrics in all the songs really meant. Like me, he had been married before. I have no children. Nicholas has two, but they live abroad with their mother. Since he's Greek Orthodox and I'm Jewish, we decided to have a civil ceremony but I was determined that the event would be both as romantic and spiritual as the way Nicholas and I feel about each other.

"Although we sent out hundreds of announcements, we invited only fifteen people to the wedding. I wrote on the announcements 'No gifts, please,' because I didn't want people who weren't invited to the wedding to be put in the position of having to send an obligatory present. The invitations were handwritten on very formal stationery. I wanted every little detail to fit the tone of romantic elegance.

"I arrived at the old-world-style hotel where we had reserved a suite in a hansom cab hired especially for the occasion. There was a table formally set for the wedding guests in the yellow and white shades which I had chosen for the wedding's color scheme. My dress was an egg-shell white, wide-sleeved, embroidered with applique flowers.

"All the guests stood in a circle around us. The judge, an old friend of mine, officiated, but his role was kept to a minimum. The real ceremony was Nicholas and I exchanging our own vows in front of our friends. After the ceremony, we dined and an orchestra played chamber music throughout the meal. When the guests left, Nicholas and I spent the night in the suite's four-poster bed before leaving on our honeymoon to Rio the next day."

Bicoastal Receptions

Remember Sally, the second-time bride who converted to her husband's Jewish faith? A tall, athletic-looking woman with a cheerful, no-nonsense air about her, Sally talked about her wedding to David.

"It was in the same synagogue where I was converted, and the setting, therefore, intensified the experience for me, spiritually as well as emotionally," Sally explained. "Both sets of kids were there and the religious quality to the ceremony was a cementing factor for our new family.

"The reception was held in the synagogue's social hall," Sally continued. "It wasn't the most glamorous room in the world, but I had a florist who transformed some very prosaic poles into extraordinarily lovely floral sculptures. Although David and I won't be having a kosher home, the sit-down dinner was done by a kosher caterer and the band played a lot of Israeli folk songs for dancing. All of David's family was at the wedding, as were most of his friends from his childhood in Brooklyn. My parents came in from San Francisco, and we also invited the friends I've made in the fifteen years I've lived in Manhattan. But there were a lot of people important to me who weren't there, such as other members of my family who couldn't make the trip to New York and all the friends I'd had growing up in San Francisco and the ones I made when I was a college student in California.

"It was to share my new marriage with those old friends and relatives that David and I had a second wedding reception —in San Francisco. We had a cocktail party at the top of the Mark Hopkins Hotel, where there was a dazzling view of the whole city at sunset. My children came along so that they could be a part of my reunion with my youth at the same time that David met many of the people who were so important to me when I was growing up.

"I would strongly recommend two receptions," Sally concluded, "for those couples who come from opposite ends of the country and want to share the joy of their marriage on both coasts."

Sentiment and Space

Peg and Rick combined the sweetness of sentiment with the advantages of space when they split up their wedding ceremony and reception. The ceremony was held in the small apartment of the friends who had introduced them by inviting them both to dinner there. A few family members and a handful of close friends were present to witness the minister marry the couple. Then everyone joined in a champagne toast provided by the host and hostess, who were responsible for bringing them together.

Following the bubbly salutation, the small wedding party departed for a huge loft owned by other friends of the bride and groom, who threw a reception to which over a hundred people were invited. The bridal couple provided a catered buffet supper and full bar for their many friends. Several musician friends donated their services for an evening in which the guests rocked and rolled far into the night.

Winter Paradise

Another couple wanted to celebrate their marriage in a place which had romantic significance for them. Bart and Phyllis were both architects, had worked for the same firm for several years, and had become good friends before romance bloomed between them. Because Bart had custody of the children from his first marriage, which had ended in a complicated divorce, and Phyllis shared a crowded apartment with her three daughters, the new couple had difficulty finding time to be alone. The first time they were by themselves was on a winter weekend trip to a sprawling country inn in the Berkshire Mountains. Those two days and nights, away from responsibilities of work and children, enabled them to relax, and their feelings for each other ripened.

Almost a year later, following a stressful period of problems with ex-spouses and with their employers, who questioned their staying at the same firm now that they were engaged, Bart and Phyllis were ready to get married. Since it was close to the time of year when they had gone on their romantic weekend, they decided to hold their wedding at the same country inn. Phyllis and Bart took rooms for fifteen friends and family members and made all the necessary transportation arrangements. The ceremony was held in front of a roaring fire in the inn's colonial-style drawing room. The couple was married by the local justice of the peace. They then invited the wedding party to a full-course New England dinner in the dining room, after which brandy and coffee were served by the fireplace.

The next morning, guests took the children tobogganing on a nearby mountain while the newlyweds lingered in bed in the same room in which they had stayed on their former visit to the inn.

The bride's brother hosted a wedding luncheon in the inn's Elizabethan taproom, after which the whole wedding party had a frolic in the freshly fallen snow. The bridal couple then went off for a honeymoon at a Vermont ski chalet while the rest of the party drove back home in several cars, taking both sets of children with them. Everyone at the wedding still remembers the beautiful setting and the fun had by all the guests. And for Bart and Phyllis it will always be a very private and personal paradise, which they were lucky enough to share with those closest to them.

Back to Nature

In the sixties, back-to-nature weddings were very popular and they still have an appeal for many outdoor types. If you and your fiancé are devotees of Mother Nature, think about having your wedding in her backyard, be it the flowering meadow of a friend's country property or a windswept mountaintop. Should this idea strongly appeal to both of you, pursue it in stages. First, let your fantasies flow wherever they take you, be it woodland or seashore or rugged terrain. After determining which type of natural beauty setting is the one for your wedding, it's time to get down to specifics.

The site you finally select should offer both enough privacy to provide the serenity you seek and sufficient accessibility to satisfy practical considerations. If you know someone who owns waterfront property or a wooded area which has not yet fallen to the developer's bulldozer, ask if you can hold your nuptials there. If such a site is unavailable, or is not exactly what you have in mind, check the state park facilities and regulations in your area.

If you have settled on a remote site for your wedding in the wilderness, you'll want to make some careful provisions beforehand so that unanticipated inconveniences don't mar the occasion. Be considerate of your guests. They should be supplied with a detailed map and facts about parking facilities. If a strenuous walk along wooded trails is necessary to get to the site, the wedding invitation should include this information. People should be told to wear appropriate shoes, carry sweaters in case the air turns chilly, bring blankets if they're going to be sitting on the ground, and take flashlights with them if the nuptials are going to run into the evening. Whoever is officiating at the ceremonies needs to be apprised of these particulars.

Don't rule out the possibility of rain in your preparations. Make sure shelter is provided within the vicinity of the wedding site by a cabin, barn, tent, or other roofed location. Have some umbrellas along to offer guests, and don't forget plastic covers for the food. And speaking of food, offering something to eat and drink at your wilderness wedding will take thorough planning. Whether it's a light snack or an elaborate gourmet picnic, remember that coolers are essential for perishable foods and for beverages. Easy-to-pack plastic wineglasses not only are convenient for serving vino but will do well for beer and sodas, too. Nice touches like cushions to sit on and cloth napkins can make for a gracious atmosphere in a natural setting. These shouldn't be forgotten on your list of essentials, which will include eating implements and crucial sundries like bottle openers.

You might want to include gardening shears for cutting wild flowers to make an impromptu bridal bouquet. You could also bring baskets in which to hold the wild flowers other women in your wedding party can carry. When it comes to music in the wilderness, portable battery-operated tape decks are always feasible. But for more authenticity, you could provide easily transportable instruments for any amateur musicians among your guests. Guitars, violins, flutes, and miniature organs all make for both beautiful music and light traveling.

The more extensive your prior planning, the more perfect will be your wilderness wedding. Whether the ceremony is performed beside a quiet lake at dusk, on a glorious expanse of beach at sunset, or atop a mountain at high noon, it can be a profound experience for everyone present. Advance planning will make the occasion as pleasant as it is awesome, and your guests will be as comfortable as they are inspired.

Thematic Settings

Sometimes a setting can suggest a central theme for the wedding. This happened with Alice and Peter, who jointly owned a big old house in Illinois prior to their marriage.

The theme of the wedding was inspired by the presence of

a Renaissance fair held every year in their county. The wedding party were able to rent costumes and hire musicians, jugglers, and jesters from the fair. Alice's friends read up on the food of the period and did a good replication of a fourteenth-century feast. Alice's new stepchildren were enchanted with their costumes and the antics of jugglers and jesters. The bride wore a brightly colored gown trimmed with costume jewelry and an elaborate headdress. She carried sheaves of golden wheat, a fertility symbol back in Elizabethan England. The groom was dashing in tights, tunic, and a sword at his belt.

Another wedding theme grew out of a setting when Doug and Elaine accepted the offer of Elaine's best friend and her husband to host their nuptials. The friends owned a town house which they had decorated with authentic Victorian pieces. Elaine, a teacher of English literature whose favorite poet was Elizabeth Barrett Browning, warmed to the idea of using a Victorian motif for her wedding. She wore a Victorian lace wedding dress and veil, and persuaded Doug to wear clothes from the period. Their host and hostess also wore Victorian costumes, and several of the guests simulated that style of dress. The British theme continued into the honeymoon, where the newlyweds spent a week at an Edwardian hotel in London, and another week touring the English countryside.

A theme of a very different nature occurred to Marge and Jeff, both statisticians living and working in Washington, D.C., whose wedding was held in their friends' West Virginia vacation house.

"We did it up real country," the city-born-and-bred Marge recalled. "We had a band with a banjo, a guitar, and a fiddle playing bluegrass to which everyone danced two-steps and square dances. We roasted a pig and served baked beans, potato salad, and homemade coleslaw accompanied by a keg of beer and jugs of hard cider. We were married by the closest thing you can find to an old-fashioned backwoods preacher in this day and age. All our academically oriented friends from Washington said it was the best wedding they'd ever been to."

Private Clubs

For those who don't want an at-home wedding but feel a hotel or catering hall is too impersonal, private clubs offer convenience and a personal touch. Suburban country clubs can provide stylish settings for nuptial celebrations while urban ones, often situated in stately town houses, give an aura of elegance to any wedding. If you are a member of such a club, there is no problem having your wedding there, provided you clear the date sufficiently ahead of time. If you don't belong to one but are eligible for membership, you might consider joining. Many prominent universities have clubs in major cities, and if you or your fiancé is a graduate of one of these institutions, you can become a member.

Perhaps you have friends who could propose your name for membership in their club. If you don't have the time or interest in such a membership prior to the wedding, check on which clubs will permit nonmembers to hold weddings on their premises. In this case, too, having a friend who is a member can be very helpful.

"I had never thought about joining the country club near my house because I'm neither a golf nor a tennis player, but it did look like the perfect setting for a wedding," said Bettina, a second-time bride living and working in the suburbs. "When I discussed this possibility with my neighbors, who are members of the club, they arranged for the wedding to be held there under their sponsorship."

Local Color

"We wanted a wedding site with charm and character but had just moved into a high-rise condo not especially strong in those two areas," said Sandy, a guidance counselor in Austin, Texas, marrying an accountant. They found their ideal location in one of the beautiful parks of their own city. From New

York's magnificent Botanical Gardens to the Seattle Aquarium, American cities offer an intriguing range of wedding sites. Over two thousand such options are listed in *Places*, a nationwide directory of public places for private events and private places for public functions. This invaluable source book can be found at many public libraries or ordered directly from P.O. Box 810, Gracie Station, New York, N.Y. 10028 (212-737-7536). The price of the directory is $18.95, which includes postage, taxes, and handling charges (add $1.50 for First Class or Air Mail). Checks or money orders are to be made out to Tenth House, Enterprises, Inc.

Places is divided by regions, and along with the description of each site is a photograph, an exact address, and a phone number to call. Information is also provided about how large a party can be accommodated, and whether or not there is a resident caterer available. Prices are not given in the directory but can easily be obtained by a phone call or inquiring letter. The prices vary from as little as five hundred dollars to as much as seventy-five hundred dollars for a four-hour period. This directory is highly recommended to any bride and groom searching for somewhere truly special for a wedding. In our rapidly homogenizing culture, regional distinctions have an appeal for those whose sense of style runs toward the unique and whose feel for local traditions is strong.

For residents of the Boston area who are steeped in New England history, a "Boston Tea Party" wedding is available on a ship in Boston Harbor, which is a full-size working replica of one of the three original "Tea Party" ships. Guests can join in the spirit of the occasion by hauling cargo overboard while the crew chants the rallying cry which ignited the American Revolution. As particular to New York as the "Tea Party" is to Boston is the "Streets of New York Buffet," a party thrown at the World Trade Center featuring the uniquely diverse culinary specialties of the Big Apple. Live music is included.

Residents of the Mid-Atlantic states might be interested in a novel wedding party idea in Maryland. A private company has bought up an old railroad line and completely refurbished its Art Deco railroad cars, which can be chartered for short runs. Lovejoy Plantation in Lovejoy, Georgia, just twenty miles from Atlanta, deep in *Gone With the Wind* country, is an antebellum mansion, set on twelve hundred acres of working plantation and decorated with Confederate memorabilia and antiques. The resident caterer offers a specialty called Magnolia Suppers and can accommodate as many as a thousand guests at outdoor barbecues. If you ever had girlhood fantasies of being Scarlett O'Hara, here's your grown-up chance to do just that.

You can hold your wedding party in a fourteen-room Federalist house in Louisville, Kentucky, which was built after a design by Thomas Jefferson. In Asheville, North Carolina, there is the Blue Ridge Mountain House, once the Vanderbilt estate, designed in the style of a French Renaissance chateau. In Milwaukee, the Flemish Renaissance castle built by a brewery baron would make a fanciful site for a wedding celebration. For those whose historical imagination is captivated by the Wild West, there is the Patee House Museum in Kansas City. Run by the Pony Express Historical Association, this former luxury hotel is rich in Western lore, especially so since Jesse James frequented the place.

California has many wedding sites with a strong regional flavor. In the northern part of the state, there is the Winery in Windsor, California, a modern vineyard located in the Russian River Valley, an hour and a half's drive from San Francisco. The winery has a banquet room and two patios as well as a theater. For a particularly picturesque wedding party, you could try the Victorian Lighthouse in San Francisco Bay.

Los Angeles, of course, offers its own inimitable possibilities for a wedding party. In Hollywood, there is the Dream Factory, a museum of movie memorabilia where your guests can wander amid the sets, props, and costumes of their favorite films. For a more specialized Hollywood dream come true, you can charter the boat which once belonged to John Wayne.

A converted World War II mine sweeper, it is now a 140-foot yacht in mint condition. Let the resident caterer and crew arrange for your wedding party to enjoy a cruise along Long Beach Harbor, where you can dance in the star's pleasure vessel.

A special treat awaits animal lovers in Escondido, California, located midway between Los Angeles and San Diego. This is the home of the San Diego Wild Animal Park run by the San Diego Zoological Society. Here, on 1,800 acres of sanctuary, animals can roam in settings similar to their natural homeland. Tentlike sites are available for wedding receptions. There is also a very special site for wedding ceremonies on Pumzika Point, which means "Peaceful Outlook" in Swahili. The Point is located on the Hiking Trail and has a wooden edifice overlooking acres of animals freely roaming the fields.

After looking through *Places*, you may be inspired to hold your wedding somewhere rich in regional traditions and historical associations. You may also live in a community which does not provide for wedding parties in such locations. Here's where you can use some social and civic know-how, should you be so motivated. Contact your town's historical society and see if, for instance, a mansion significant in local lore is open for tours. If so, you might suggest opening it to wedding parties—starting with yours. Perhaps you could interest an influential restaurant owner in catering the party, and enlist his help in persuading the historical society to give your idea a try. Should you have good contacts with members of your Chamber of Commerce, your suggestions will be taken that much more seriously.

Such a course of action would certainly be in keeping with the innovative energy you are bringing to your new marriage. In selecting a setting for your wedding party, be as flexible and creative as possible. It's good practice for the way you'll want to live your newly married life.

Going Abroad

Another alternative exists for those couples with family and friends spread across both coasts. Take off on a romantic wedding trip for just the two of you.

"It was all getting so complicated," said Marcie, thirty-two, a divorced manager of a credit company. "My parents live in Kansas, his in Maine, and we live in Oregon. Old family grievances were erupting all over the place and I didn't want to have to deal with all that again, having gone through a series of family feuds which got my first marriage off to a bad start. Since Todd and I were planning a honeymoon in Italy, we just decided to get married while we were there."

Marcie and Todd found that although they had to deal with considerable red tape and phone calls to the State Department, "those hassles weren't fraught with the emotional complications of family disputes and so were easier to deal with."

To marry abroad requires passports, birth certificates, and a divorce decree, if there has been a previous marriage. The consulate of the country in which you wish to be married can be extremely helpful, as can a travel agent. Most couples who persevere through the bureaucratic hurdles find the rewards well worth it. In combining the wedding and the honeymoon, you can save money, families and friends are more easily placated since one locale hasn't been chosen over another, and finally, there is the romance of a wedding and a honeymoon in an exotic place.

If you're seriously considering a wedding abroad, make a list of several countries in which you would like to marry. Then check their requirements with the consulate. Choose a country whose rules are manageable for you, as well as one which you find appealing for your marriage. Here are some facts to consider in making your preliminary list:

Italy requires a notarized document that one is single and free to marry.

Mexico insists on a chest X ray among other medical tests.

France requires a civil ceremony as well as a religious one. Since the civil ceremony requires a thirty-day residency period, it can be easier to have it performed in the United States, and then you can have a French religious ceremony.

Many countries require that documents be registered at a government office at least one week before the ceremony.

Spain requires proof that you are free to marry, and for a church wedding, a baptismal certificate is necessary.

If you are undaunted by these obstacles and are already thinking about a European or Mexican honeymoon, a foreign wedding could be an option for you. If you are planning a summer wedding, you might want to consider Scotland with its magnificent countryside and no residency requirement. Italy, of course, is a sheer delight, especially in early autumn or late spring when the weather is warm but the tourists haven't yet invaded the country. The famous Italian spirit of sociability can turn a simple civil ceremony into a festive occasion, with the staffs of marriage bureaus presenting gifts to the surprised bride and groom.

If, on the other hand, you are planning a winter wedding and looking forward to a Caribbean honeymoon, it is easier to combine the wedding and honeymoon. Jamaica, Puerto Rico, and the U.S. Virgin Islands are particularly relaxed about residency requirements. Some couples who are getting married in the Caribbean and have friends also planning a Caribbean holiday arrange to fly there together. This way, you get an exotic foreign wedding with a slight touch of home.

For the epitome of exotic combined with a simple set of

requirements, you can't beat getting married in Maui. The loveliest of the enchanting Hawaiian Islands, the place is a honeymoon paradise. Combining the wedding and honeymoon in this magical setting is tempting indeed. There's no waiting period for the eight-dollar license issued by the State Department of Health in Honolulu and agents in Maui. It's valid for a thirty-day period throughout Hawaii. The only stipulation is that women must present a certificate confirming premarital screening for rubella.

Once these brief formalities are out of the way, you are free to choose where on Maui your marriage will take place. You can look into the attractive wedding packages offered by the large hotels and condos. Or you can choose from one of the world's most lavish array of outdoor settings. A tropical meadow overlooking the ocean is one option; chartering a yacht for the ceremony is another. Helicopters will take you to hidden beaches and secluded waterfalls where you can exchange your vows in settings of breathtaking beauty and incomparable privacy. Some intrepid couples have even had their marriage ceremony performed on the summit of Haleakala, the world's largest dormant volcano whose sunrise views provide a visual pilgrimage for visitors to Maui.

If this "away from it all" option whets your romantic appetite, information can be obtained from foreign consulates which are located in most major American cities. The State Department's Bureau of Consular Affairs can also be helpful, as can the Caribbean Tourism Association located in New York City. So, bon voyage!

CHAPTER SEVEN

What's in a Name?

What's in a name? Only your identity, or at least the most apparent symbol of it. Less than twenty years ago, women almost invariably assumed their husband's name upon marrying. Even those few who were too well known professionally by their maiden name to change it for business purposes elected to use the husband's surname in private life. There was no Ms. which saw you through a lifetime. You were Miss till a man came along and made you his Mrs. While the days of Miss Mary Jones being transformed on her wedding day into Mrs. John Smith are gone forever, last names remain a problem for many people. Here are a few solutions, some of which might work well for you.

Ms. Forever

Women whose first marriage took place in the late seventies or early eighties often retained their maiden name in keeping with the advancements the women's movement had made. If you fall into this category, then as far as the world is concerned, you never had a last name other than the one with which you were born. You may want to proceed the same way in your second marriage, but there are exceptions to this pattern. Very often, women who never took their husband's name the first time around decide to do so in their second marriages. Their reasons vary from the symbolic to the social to the practical.

"I'm feeling more traditional than I did when I married the first time," said a woman in her late thirties whose first marriage began and ended before she was twenty-five. "I feel more committed this time, and I think taking my husband's name is a way of clarifying that commitment."

Another divorced woman, Lauren, also in her thirties and the mother of two children, is marrying a widower who is a respected member of a conservative community into which she is eager to be accepted. "It might be different if my children and I had the same last name but we don't because I used my maiden name throughout my first marriage and they have their father's name, so this won't be any change for them," Lauren explained. "Actually, it will be easier for my kids this way because their mother and their stepfather will have the same name, so they'll only have to explain two different names rather than three at their new school."

Betty, a second-time bride who still has her maiden name, is taking her new husband's because they are going into business together and "it's much more convenient that way," she explained. "Some of my very feminist friends resent what I'm doing," she added, "but I've become more pragmatic, less theoretical than I used to be. For us, it works better and that's all I care about."

Middle Initials

The name game is more complicated for women who did take their husband's name when they first married.

"I married when I was still in graduate school, in the late sixties," said Peggy, an associate professor in her mid-forties and the mother of two college students. "I switched to my husband's name without giving it a second thought."

When Peggy's marriage ended in divorce fourteen years later, she kept her married name, as do so many women after a divorce from a marriage in which they had children. Even those who don't have children often keep their first husband's name if they have used it long enough to build up a professional reputation. Peggy's feelings on the subject are mixed. "On the one hand, I dislike continuing to have the name of a man about whom I still feel very bitter, but the reality is that I have published a dissertation, two academic books, and scores of articles in professional journals under my first married name. To change it now would not be a smart career move, so I'll keep it even though it does rankle."

Another woman is keeping her first husband's name, although changing to her new husband's name would not adversely affect her career as a schoolteacher. "I went through the hassle of changing my identity once, and then when I saw younger women keeping their maiden name, I resented having made the change," she remembers. "Now I just don't feel like changing it, when a man keeps the same name for his whole life."

"It's as though my first married name is my maiden name," said Leah, who was married to her first husband for nearly twenty years and now, in her mid-forties, is getting married again.

"I will be taking my new husband's name," she said firmly. "But the name on the wedding announcements is my first husband's. I haven't used my maiden name for almost a quarter of a century and no one where I now live has ever known me by it. It just doesn't make sense to resurrect it now." Leah is buying new linens and towels for her second marriage and they are all monogrammed with the initials of her first name, her first husband's last name, and her second husband's last name. "It seems kind of crazy but it's the most workable solution I can come up with."

A.K.A.

Donna kept her maiden name, Nichols, for business reasons following her first marriage, but in her children's school, local civic organizations, and the shopping mall, she was known by her husband's name, Hanson. For the sake of clarity, Donna had her checks printed with the following names:

> *Donna Nichols*
> *a.k.a. Donna Hanson*

"Sometimes I looked at my checks and felt like I should be on the Most Wanted List," Donna quipped, but said that the "a.k.a." cut down on the confusion.

When Donna's marriage ended in divorce and she remarried a short time later, there was now a third name in her life. "At my husband's country club, with his business associates, and among his old friends, I'm Donna MacKenzie," she said with a shrug of bemusement at the complexities of it all. She and her husband have a joint checking account on which she has written all three of her last names along with his name. But on the checks for her own checking account, which she still retains to pay bills relating to her children's activities and her household expenses, the "a.k.a." remains.

"I used to be a fairly uptight person," Donna admitted, "but all this havoc in my personal life, all these name changes, have taught me 'to go with the flow.' I no longer have the expectation that everything will run like clockwork and I think I'm better off this way."

"I'm pretty relaxed about the name business by now," said thrice-married Monica Shelby. Shelby is the maiden name she resumed after her first marriage ended. But she had started a small mail-order enterprise with her first husband and kept his name for matters directly relating to that business.

"Shelby is the name on my driver's license and passport. It's the one I use for voting and jury duty," Monica said. "But when it comes to various business activities, to social connections from different periods of my life, I just use the name by which I am known in that particular circle." Monica, who has one child from her second marriage, is expecting another with her third husband. She is aware that this will create more nomenclature complications.

"To my daughter's friends and their parents, to her teachers and other school personnel, I am known by her last name," Monica explained. "I'll do the same for this baby," she added. "It all makes for a lot of confusion, but then my personal life *has* been rather messy—although not boring," she noted with a wry smile.

Not every woman has Monica's nonchalance about these matters, but most second wives do get used to misunderstandings and confusions about their names. It seems to come with the territory and, like everything else in this land of remarriage, requires a capacity for compromise. Toni Mason made a decision about using her maiden name because of strong feelings on the part of the man who was soon to be her second husband.

"Mason was my first husband's name," said Toni, a very youthful forty-year-old systems analyst. "Len, the man I'm marrying, is very angry about the rough time my first husband gave me and was really upset about my keeping his name." Toni would have taken Len's name except for the fact that she was already in a situation where she was known to some business associates by her maiden name and to others by her first husband's.

"I do a lot of consulting, so I've worked in many different places. There was enough confusion already without adding a third name to my resume," Toni felt. Her compromise is to resume her maiden name, which will appease her new husband

and keep further career complications to a minimum. "What kind of a systems analyst would I be if I couldn't solve such a relatively simple problem?"

Hyphenated Wives

Before the women's movement, hyphenated names were the province of British aristocrats and a handful of their American imitators. Then sometime in the early seventies, the vanguard of modern-day feminists began taking their maiden and married names and hyphenating them.

"I was Bonnie Sage before I married Chuck Lester in 1970," recalled a San Francisco real estate broker. "Then I joined a consciousness-raising group and became Bonnie Sage-Lester." Several years after Bonnie and Chuck Lester got divorced, she married a lawyer named Robert Myers and became known as Bonnie Lester-Myers. Why not Sage-Myers? The question was certainly one she considered before opting to hyphenate the names of both husbands and delete her maiden name.

"At first I thought of using all three but Sage-Lester-Myers sounded too much like a roll call, so I dropped the Sage because my kids are named Lester and it's a name that is more familiar to most of the people in my life than Sage," explained Bonnie.

With the complexities of contemporary life, hyphenated names for wives make a lot of sense. A second-time bride who resumed, or never relinquished, her maiden name can tack her new husband's name onto it. For those using their first husband's name, hyphenating it with the second husband's name can work well. And for those, like Bonnie, who have already hyphenated a maiden and married name, you can drop either of the first two names and add the third. The hyphenated solution cuts down on confusion and makes less explanation necessary. It can bring clarity and continuity to introductions and the renewal of old business contacts. Hyphenated names convey something of your personal history with style, efficiency, and dignity. Try writing one out for yourself and see how it looks. Now say it aloud. If the sound strikes you as right, you just may have acquired an addition to your identity.

CHAPTER EIGHT

Invitations and Announcements

Second wedding invitations can be less formal and much more individualized than those for a first wedding. The single most distinguishing characteristic of the invitation here is that, in most instances, parents are not mentioned. If you want the wording on the more formal side, the invitation could read:

Mary Jones and Jack Smith
Request the honor of your presence
At their marriage
Saturday, the first of February

Twelve o'clock noon
Union Methodist Church

Reception immediately following
The University Club

A less formal version of the same invitation might read:

Mary Jones and Jack Smith
Invite you to share in their happiness
As they unite in marriage
Saturday the first of February

Twelve o'clock noon
Union Methodist Church

Please join us at a buffet
Following the ceremony
The University Club

Here's another and even more casual phrasing of the same invitation:

We're making it official!
You can see it all happen
When Mary Jones and John Smith
Become a married couple

Saturday, February 1, at noon

Lunch with us afterward
At the University Club

Even if the wedding is being given at the home of a friend, the invitation can still come from the couple themselves:

Mary Jones and John Smith
Invite you to our wedding
At the home of Tom and Nancy Reardon
Saturday, February 1

Join us for lunch
Following the noon ceremony

Your invitation should convey the tone as well as impart the facts about the wedding. If you are holding it at your mother's home but you and your fiancé are doing all the planning and financing, let the invitation reflect your independence:

Mary Jones and John Smith
Invite you to celebrate our marriage
At the home of Evelyn and Roger Jones
Saturday, the first of February

Lunch will follow the noon ceremony

There is a difference between a parent or friend offering their home for your wedding, and their giving you the wedding. If someone is giving you the wedding, then it is appropriate for the invitation to come from the host and hostess:

Tom and Nancy Reardon
Invite you to celebrate
The marriage of Mary Jones and John Smith

Saturday, the first of February

Join us for lunch
Following the ceremony at high noon

In the most cases, though, the invitation will come directly from the bride and groom in whatever phrasing they prefer.

Unless your second wedding is very traditional, you can dispense with the formalities of engraved invitations enclosed in inner envelopes and separate RSVP cards. One envelope will do, and the RSVP can be written at the bottom of the invitation, followed by a phone number. For a more informal and personal style than standard printed invitations, you can write them by hand. Handwritten invitations are practical when you are asking only a small number of people to the wedding. If you're inviting so many people that writing out the invitations is too time-consuming a chore but you like the look of the invitation in your own hand, write out one and take it to a printer. He can print copies of your handwritten original.

Should your aesthetic sense be more refined than your handwriting, think about hiring the services of a professional calligrapher. Look through the calligrapher's samples till you find the one which looks best to you. Many calligraphers offer packages which include the selection and purchase of your stationery. Another alternative is to find someone you know who has an elegant penmanship. Perhaps you or your fiancé has a child with a gracefully flowing hand who might offer to address the envelopes as a wedding present.

If you are asking a limited number of guests to the ceremony and a much larger group to the reception, you could send out two sets of invitations. A printed invitation would invite people to the reception. Those you want to have present at your ceremony could receive the printed invitation to the reception along with a highly personalized handwritten invitation asking them to attend the ceremony as well. If you are asking only about a dozen people to the ceremony, a letter on your personal stationery could be sent to each one, telling why that individual is important to you and how much his or her presence at the ceremony would mean to you and your fiancé. If your fiancé is not up to writing such missives, you could write them, telling Aunt Emily how fondly Tom always speaks of her, etc. It's a nice touch and adds that extra dimension of warmth with which you want to suffuse your wedding.

Whether written on your personal notepaper, or printed on formal cards, your invitations can be as much a statement about you, as much a reflection of your particular wedding style, as the clothes you wear and the reception you plan. Don't be afraid to choose something vibrant when picking colors for paper and ink. There's no need to confine yourself to classic shades of ecru, buff, or pastel blue. How about a bright green ink on a heavy vellum paper, or a vibrant azure ink on ivory paper? You can have exotic colors of ink printed on a dark paper, such as grape, magenta, or turquoise. Instead of combining lavender and gray, think about how striking a dark gray ink on peach or rose paper could look. Don't be timid about experimenting with exotic combinations.

When you shop for stationery, take along a friend with a flair for the flamboyant. Study different styles of type, or a calligrapher's portfolio, until you find style which pleases you. It needn't be neat, precise lettering. A bold scrawl might well be more expressive of the mood in which you are sailing into your new lifestyle.

If you're handwriting wedding invitations, you could do it on joint stationery, using the first person plural. Order stationery whose letterhead contains both your names instead of automatically separating all your correspondence into *his* and *hers*.

After you've sent out the invitations, you may want to think about wedding announcements. If you are going to send announcements, they should be mailed within a day or two of the wedding. If they're mailed much afterward, they seem to be correcting an oversight. If they're sent a few weeks before the wedding, the recipient may confuse the announcement with an invitation. It's not always necessary to send announcements, and doing so shouldn't be done routinely. An announcement is to inform people who have not been invited to the wedding of your marriage. If just about everyone you know has been invited, you may not need to send announcements. Or if there are just a handful of friends and relatives who live far away, you could write personal letters or make some long-distance phone calls.

In most cases, however, printed announcements are a practical way of telling people whom you're not inviting to the wedding about your marriage. The announcement can also be a way of letting people know which of several possible names you have chosen, and your new address.

Newspaper announcements are a long-standing tradition for first weddings and you are free to send your local paper an announcement of your second marriage. Some of the newspapers in large cities charge a fee for the announcement, others do not. If no fee is charged, there is no guarantee that the announcement will be printed. All the big-city papers have guidelines for writing the announcement which indicate the information they wish included, routine facts such as the date and place of the wedding, addresses, alma maters, and occupations of the bride and groom and similar background data on their parents.

Only the New York *Times* of all the major national newspapers insists on information about the previous marriages of the bridal couple, and whether those marriages were terminated by death or divorce. The *Times*'s society editor will not say what percentage of received announcements are printed, but among status-conscious New Yorkers it is important to be one of the elite whose announcements *do* reach print. The *Times* is chillingly vague about their criteria but it seems to have a lot to do with family background as well as the achievements of the betrothed couple. The Chicago *Sun Times* charges $30 for a wedding announcement. Neither the Los Angeles *Times* nor the Boston *Globe* charges for the space, but the Washington *Post* does.

Those papers which don't charge for the announcement say they will print it if space permits. Obviously, when space is at a premium, social prominence is a major factor in deciding whose announcement gets to see the light of day. But the competition isn't as fierce, nor the prize so eagerly sought, outside New York City. Smaller cities usually print every announcement they receive even though it may take them a little extra time to do so if there are a lot of announcements coming in at once, as is always the case in June. If you're from a town where wedding announcements are run on a casual basis but you now live in a metropolis, you might want to send the announcement to the paper of your hometown if your family still lives there. Seeing your name on their local society page could be a pleasant treat for your parents.

Besides the newspaper announcement and the printed announcement, certain situations call for more specialized announcements. If, for instance, you've opted for a wedding abroad at which no one you know will be present, you might want to do a large mailing on your return to inform everyone that you are now married. While the facts simply printed will suffice, more creative options are available.

When one enterprising bride returned from a combined wedding-honeymoon in Italy with her new husband, she took a blank piece of paper, a black Magic Marker, and scrawled the following letter:

To Our Many Friends,

Jonathan and I were married in Rome on May 3rd and followed the ceremony with a glorious drive through Tuscany. We'd long dreamed of a trip to Italy and we decided to combine it with a wedding. We're still living in the same apartment, but are in the process of buying a house in the suburbs so that there will be more room when Jonathan's children come to visit. We're planning a huge open house when we do make the move and will let you know the details later. For now, we just want to tell you of our new marital status and our deep happiness.

With much love,
Mary Walters-Katz and Jonathan Katz

Mary then bought a hundred sheets of pink-colored paper with matching envelopes and took her letter to a copy shop, which ran it off for her on the pink sheets. She and her children and her new husband's kids spent the weekend addressing and stamping envelopes, and after mailing the announcements, the newlyweds took all the kids out to the horror movie of their choice to thank them for their help.

Another bride left the wedding announcements up to her new husband, a computer buff. Her wedding present to him had been a graphics card for his personal computer. He used it to write up an announcement of their nuptials with multicolored letters. The written words were accompanied by a drawing of a balding groom carrying a beaming bride over the threshold, or rather across the vestibule of the brownstone in which they had both been living for several years.

One bride who lives in Los Angeles wrote a charmingly zany, rather raunchy announcement of her third marriage to all her acquaintances whom she couldn't invite to the wedding. But she didn't feel this off-beat style would go over too well in her Minnesota hometown, so she sent conventionally worded announcements to everyone she knew there. She also had an announcement run in her hometown newspaper, so that anyone who wasn't on her list for mailed announcements but might be interested in the news was informed of her recent nuptials.

Some couples send out announcements on mock telegram stationery, and others have their own cards made up. One couple designed a particularly striking announcement on thick cream-colored cards, with a cover printed in violet ink that said, "Hear ye, Hear ye!" Inside was a handwritten announcement, signed by both bride and groom.

Poems, lines from songs, and zippy anecdotes can be included in your announcement if you choose. Whatever you do depends on personal taste, and the circumstances of your wedding. If there were very few people at your wedding, then a less formal, more unique announcement is appropriate because it will go to many of your close friends. But if most of your friends were at the wedding and the announcement is for business associates, casual acquaintances, and relatives with whom you are not in frequent contact, a more standard announcement might be better. Or you can always try sending two versions.

One couple who did this were Hank and Jane. Partners in the publication of technical manuals, they were at a sales convention in Nevada when they impulsively got married there. Upon their return, they sent out two sets of announcements.

One was a formal printed card, mostly to business contacts. The other was for their friends, and was a combined announcement card and invitation to a big open house the newlyweds were throwing the following month.

Whatever innovations you choose for invitations and announcements, keep one thing in mind: Each has separate functions. The first is to invite; the second, to inform. Invitations should be proffered and information imparted in a style that is uniquely yours. They should make the same striking and pleasing impression you pride yourself on making in person.

CHAPTER NINE

Guest Lists

It is over the guest list that families often have their fiercest fights in a first wedding. "It was a nightmare," recalled Nadine, who married for the first time the summer between her sophomore and junior years at college. "My parents were paying for the whole wedding and they invited all of their relatives, lots of their friends, and many of my father's business associates. When my fiancé's mother complained that so few of her family and friends were being asked, I told my mother, who promptly called his mother and a whole feud started."

If your first wedding guest list caused anywhere near the grievances Nadine's did, you'll be as determined as she was to avoid this happening for the second wedding. "This time it's *my* list, I mean *ours*," Nadine hastily corrected herself. The correction is well worth noting. Since this second wedding is as much your future husband's as it is yours, you had best write out the guest list together, just the two of you. Then resolve any discrepancies between you and present a united front to the rest of the world. You'll find that just between you two, there are enough differences of opinion to be a potential source of resentment without even bringing anyone else into it.

To make your planning easier, divide the possible guests into four groups: family, friends, colleagues, and exes. Then make a list for each one, putting question marks by names neither of you agree on. Expect some clashes of opinions, and talk them out till you reach a solution with which you can both be happy. Not so easy? Neither is having a successful marriage. Making a workable guest list and achieving a mutually rewarding life both have the same cornerstone—communication—so study the question marks on your list and share your reservations, honestly and lovingly. Let's take a look at your list.

Family

For purposes of this discussion, family will refer to the ones you and he were born into. The ones either of you may have made in a previous marriage do not fall into this category.

"My mother simply assumed I'd be inviting all my aunts, uncles, and cousins, just the way we had asked them to my first wedding," said thirty-six-year-old Patti. "But Larry and I had decided we wanted a very small wedding. Aside from our parents, siblings, and their spouses, we were going to be inviting only friends, no other family. I had already explained to my mother when we became engaged that this wedding would be different from the first, that Larry and I would be making all the decisions. She understood our feelings perfectly, in the abstract. But when it came down to the reality that her sisters wouldn't be asked to her daughter's wedding, my mother became extremely upset."

Patti's experience is typical of the parental opposition many independent women face over the guest list for a second wedding. No matter how much parents concede in principle on the right of the bride and groom to ask whom they choose, when it comes down to specifics, conflicts are apt to erupt. The ensuing conversations don't always run as smoothly and sweetly as you would like.

"Putting together the second wedding dredged up a lot of bad feelings between me and my mother over my first wedding," said Jeanette, a graphics designer in her early thirties. Jeanette had married for the first time the same June that she'd graduated from college. "I always wondered if my mother was aware of all the doubts I had about the wedding even then," Jeanette said. It was only when planning her second wedding that Jeanette was able to ask her mother that question. It turned out that they both had had their doubts—the young woman too unsure of herself to back out of a decision about which she was apprehensive, the mother doing her best to make everything perfect, while harboring a feeling of unease too vague to express.

Raw emotions which were buried rather than resolved between you and your parents during your first marriage may surface at this time. "Why weren't you more supportive when I told you I was leaving Steve?" Roberta, another second-time bride, finally asked her father. Now that she was getting married again, Roberta wanted to better understand how her father had felt at the time of the breakup of her first marriage.

"I didn't want you to be a divorced woman raising two children," was his answer.

"That was the most intimate talk we ever had," Roberta noted.

Not all the conversations with your parents will be this intense. More likely, they will run along the lines of, "What do you mean, you're *not* inviting Aunt Bessie to the wedding. She's *my sister*," your mother may say with real hurt in her eyes and an indignation which manages to intimidate and enrage you at the same time. If this happens, be as calm and kind as you can, but stay firm. Who said this was going to be easy?

What if you could never stand Aunt Bessie but have always had a soft spot in your heart for Aunt Sadie? Just remember that there's no right and wrong in this kind of decision. You go with what makes you feel the most comfortable, or the least uncomfortable. If you've made a decision that you're inviting only your parents and siblings, you can do something else for Aunt Sadie, such as taking her out for a special luncheon or having her to a festive dinner the week you get back from your honeymoon. Or you can follow your feelings, inviting Aunt Sadie and not Aunt Bessie. Or you can lose your nerve and ask both of them.

Don't look for parity in these tricky issues. If your fiancé was practically raised by his uncle and you have had little contact with yours, it's his who gets the invitation. You're not doing a genealogy table where every generational line has to receive the same treatment. You're dealing with human feelings, where the label of a relationship often doesn't describe its quality.

It helps to keep a sense of balance. Even if you've taken a stand on how this is *your* wedding, there may be someone who will be so deeply, needlessly hurt by the lack of an invitation that you don't want to be the cause of that kind of pain regardless of your position on the makeup of the guest list. The only guidepost you can use is to have your decisions dictated by issues of real feelings rather than petty questions of protocol and other superficialities, which have no place in as heartfelt an occasion as your second wedding.

Friends

If you're planning a large, informal reception, there's no need to get picky about *real* friends versus mere acquaintances. But if it's a smallish guest list for a pricey sit-down dinner, you've got some sorting out to do. It may have been easier the first time around, when you had only one best friend, several runners-up for second place, plus a few for third. Now there are friends with whom you were once close, with whom you've lost touch, have less in common. There are business associates with whom you've recently struck up a significant friendship, and there are others who no longer work in your office but you still feel close to.

Don't be surprised if working your way through this section of the guest list forces you to do some thinking about the role of various friendships in your life. It may also cause some friction with your fiancé. Women often have more friends than men. If he's padding his list with golf buddies while you're desperately trying to decide whom to cut from yours, there's bound to be some resentments. Another problem may come up when deciding whether single friends should be allowed to invite escorts. Should an old college friend of yours be taken off the list to make room for the very new and most probably very temporary girlfriend of your fiancé's boyhood buddy?

Wendy, a gregarious second-time bride planning a small wedding and struggling to choose between her many friends, faced just such a problem. "Bob and I finally agreed that our guests couldn't bring anyone unless it was a spouse, live-in lover, or the other half of a long-term relationship. We even used the phrase 'significant other' in the invitations," Wendy added smilingly.

Wendy's solution might work well for you, especially if your unattached women friends resent having to hunt up an escort. If, on the other hand, you have friends who would rather die than walk into a formal reception unescorted, you'll want to take their feelings into consideration. You will also want to avoid verbal wrestling matches with your friends on whether or not their man qualifies as a "significant other." Such fine distinctions notwithstanding, cutting out that automatic "and guest" from the invitation goes a long way to ensure that everyone at your wedding has a meaningful relationship, if not with you then at least with someone close to you. It may also have occurred to the born match maker in you that unescorted single men and women mix and mingle better than those with dates.

Colleagues

The old axiom that women have friends and men have colleagues probably has some contemporary validity. Since women tend to be more expressive of their emotions and more concerned with relationships than men are, it's no wonder that female friendships are often stronger than those between men.

"When we looked over our guest list and I noticed that hardly any of the names on mine was a business contact, while most of those on my fiancé's were, I realized how different our social patterns are," observed Doris, a woman who, in the dozen years since her first marriage ended in divorce, had built a whole support system around her friends. Doris made a mental note to concentrate more on professional networking and encourage the man she was marrying to make more personal friends. But that was for the future. Meanwhile, there was a guest list to finalize.

"I invited all my friends and Tom asked his closest business contacts. When we got back from our honeymoon, we threw a big party for people we know through work," Doris summed up.

If you and your fiancé are both career-oriented and have jobs for which socializing is crucial to advancement, you may decide to invite work colleagues to your wedding. There's nothing wrong with such a decision, but know what you're doing and understand that the wedding may not be the warm, intimate occasion it would be were it less office-oriented. The choice is yours.

Exes

Second weddings present special problems concerning the family and friends of former spouses. "After my father died and my mother moved to Florida, it was my in-laws I turned to when I needed help with the kids," said Betsy, a schoolteacher who remained close to her first husband's parents after her marriage broke up. When Betsy became engaged to Lew, she just assumed her children's grandparents would be coming to the wedding, but the groom objected. "Lew said that Ben's folks didn't like him, didn't accept our relationship, and that he didn't want them at our wedding," she recalled, her face expressing the confusion she had felt at that time.

Betsy insisted on asking her former in-laws to the wedding and her fiancé went along with her, but grudgingly. "Later on it turned out that the kids' grandparents didn't accept him as their stepfather, and then Lew accused me of lack of loyalty to him." It took a long time before Lew's resentments about the wedding invitation were expressed and finally resolved. A more productive way to have handled the situation, Betsy now realizes, would have been to talk to her first husband's parents before inviting them to the wedding, and find out how they felt about her new marriage and future husband.

Madelaine, a magazine editor, was engaged to a man whose best friends were the couple who had introduced him to his first wife. "This couple consistently took Frank's ex-wife's part and tried to undermine my relationship with him," Madelaine recalled, her eyes flashing with anger at the recollection. Savvy about interpersonal relations, and relentlessly honest in the expression of her opinions, Madelaine told her fiancé that she didn't want that couple at her wedding unless they could convince her of their goodwill. They couldn't, and they weren't invited.

Lynn, a young widow, sensed that her dead husband's parents irrationally resented her plans to remarry. When her fiancé told her he was reluctant to have them at the wedding, Lynn went to talk to the mother and father of the husband she had lost. Not until they had worked out their resentment and made an effort to befriend her fiancé did she invite them to the wedding.

"It hurt me to have to confront their bitterness, but I couldn't have anyone at my wedding whose presence would make my fiancé uncomfortable," Lynn said flatly.

Your first loyalty is to the man you're marrying. When it is possible to patch up differences and encourage rapprochements, by all means do so. But in a situation which isn't immediately resolvable, it is your future husband who deserves your support. Not all the friends and relatives of ex-spouses can fully accept the new marriage in time for the wedding, which doesn't mean they never will. But the wedding is yours and your fiancé's, and no one should be invited who can't rejoice in your happiness. Even if you don't agree with your fiancé's assessment of another's attitude, respect his feelings.

"My second husband didn't want my first husband's brother at our wedding, even though he was a wonderful uncle to the children," explained Susan, a very pretty second-time bride and the mother of three small boys. Although her groom insisted his predecessor's brother didn't like him, Susan was convinced that it was jealousy of the brother's resemblance to her first husband which was the root cause of the resentment. "I just gave in, respecting my fiancé's feelings, even though I thought they were off base," Susan said. She had a private chat with her former brother-in-law and explained to him why he couldn't come to the wedding. It took a while, but now the two men get along well, a happy ending Susan attributes to the fact that she didn't push an unwelcome wedding guest on the man she was marrying.

Loyalty is an essential component of a good marriage. This is not to say your marital motto will be, "My husband, right or wrong," but it does mean that your wedding is not the field on which to champion causes unpopular with the man you are marrying. A wedding is a celebratory event, not a negotiating table. Probably what each of you most requires from the other is that show of solidarity which takes precedence over previous attachments. This is not the time to hold back on a demonstration of devotion but to make it wholeheartedly. There will be time enough to work out differences with others. This is your time, and that *your* is to be taken in its plural meaning.

CHAPTER TEN

Gift Ideas

What do you give the person who has everything? That despairing question, usually asked at Christmastime, may haunt the second-time bride who feels her family and friends are irritably inquiring it of one another. Maybe you're wondering what you would give if you were they. And you may also be asking yourself if it's appropriate for you to register your gift requests at a department store's bridal gift registry just as though you were a blushing first-time bride. The answer is yes.

Gift Registry

A gift registry can be even more helpful to those shopping for a second bride than for a first one. With a first-time bride starting up housekeeping, there's a wide range of useful gifts to bestow on her. But when you already have a well-stocked household and may, in fact, be consolidating two households, your friends and relatives need all the hints they can get.

Of course you have your blender, food processor, toaster oven, etc. But since you first put together a workable kitchen, there have been new variations on old themes which you might wish to acquire. How about a new, smaller food processor, which will chop things like a single onion? Or a new ice cream maker which turns out sherbets and ice creams almost instantly? Have more specialized kinds of irons, vacuum cleaners, and coffee grinders become available since your initial purchases? The era of robots in the kitchen is still around the corner, but if you look through hardware departments of major stores, you'll probably see improvements on appliances which could make highly practical wedding presents.

If you ordered a whole new set of monogrammed towels, sheets, and pillowcases in the last year of your first marriage, these are obviously not appropriate for your second marriage, so you may want to purchase a new supply. You can pick out colors and textures at your leisure, and then register your selections. Also, tablecloths and dish towels grow worn with time and you may want to spruce up your supply. Shopping around for replacements could turn out to be a voyage of self-discovery as it dawns on you how significantly your tastes have changed since the last time you registered such items.

Department store bridal registries report they are doing a brisk business with second marriages. "These women tend to pick out gift items rather than patterns," observes one bridal registry consultant. She goes on to explain that second-time brides don't pick out china or silver patterns, because they prefer individual pieces. Crystal vases and bowls also crop up frequently on the lists of these prospective brides.

Personalized Gifts

Many second brides still feel reluctant to sign up with a bridal registry, however. "I tried to do it," said one such lady, "but I was hit with this overwhelming déjà vu feeling. All the memories of my first wedding and my unhappy marriage came back to me, and I knew there was no way I could go through with the bridal registry routine twice in one lifetime."

Other women have less violent, but equally definite, reactions to the idea. "It just seemed too coy, girlish, whatever," commented the dynamic director of a management consultant agency. "It wasn't that I was opposed to getting gifts, nor to helping my friends out with suggestions. It's just that the whole setup in the department store seemed out of synch with my personal style."

Similar sentiments were expressed by the account executive of a major advertising agency. "I prefer to let those who want to give me presents use their imaginations, or ask me directly what kind of gifts I would like. Being a very direct person, I would be much more comfortable with expressing a preference on the phone, than saying at which department store I'm registered."

If these sentiments strike a chord of recognition in you, think about how you're going to answer those friends who hint that they're in need of some tips on what to get you for a second wedding present.

"Whatever you think best" is *not* the answer you want to give in this conversation. "Oh, Sue Ann, you know how I admire your taste in pottery" is a nicely phrased hint. Remind your friends of any period pieces you collect, such as Depression glass or Art Deco dishes. Or let them know that you're buying a beach house or an alpine retreat, or redecorating your apartment in an entirely different style.

Other kinds of gifts which are appropriate for a second marriage are those based on activities and interests of the newlyweds. In this promising category could go season tickets to sporting events, to a repertory theater, or to a series of concerts. If you and your fiancé are known to enjoy working out, exercise equipment would make an excellent gift, as would a few friends getting together to buy both of you a year's membership at a health spa. If a new video rental shop has opened in your area, a membership there would be a good gift idea. So would a year's supply of special wines, fruits, or flowers delivered to your home monthly.

The more distinct your personal style, the more defined your interests, the easier it will be for family and friends to give you presents reflective of that style and those interests. If you're fond of vintage wines, rare books, or Japanese artifacts, these are all potential presents for enterprising gift givers. If you have a favorite specialty shop, such as an antique store featuring a particular period which interests you, a gift certificate to the shop might be a terrific wedding present.

Gifts of Talents

In keeping with the goal of making this second wedding warmly personal, you can suggest that friends make you a gift of their talents. The more informal your approach, the more flexible your style, the freer you will be to ask your cousin who owns a bakery to make your wedding cake, or your college roommate who's now a graphic artist to design the cover for your wedding invitations. Even your aunt the dressmaker could cut the pattern for your wedding dress from the sketch of a fashion designer friend.

Of course, you will make it clear that these offerings are to be *in lieu* of any other gift. Make sure, however, that your requests will be a source of gratification rather than resentment. If you have a copywriter friend who's frantic with on-the-job deadlines, asking her or him to help you phrase personalized invitations and announcements may be out of the question. Think through just *what* it is you are actually asking of *whom* before you barge ahead with requests for what may turn out to be time-consuming services reluctantly performed.

People are often more flattered being asked to do something at which they are eager amateurs rather than overworked professionals. Keep this in mind when you talk to friends who are caterers, photographers, and musicians. Asking an aunt who loves to cook to prepare her Swedish meatballs for your wedding reception is a far cry from requesting the same from a friend who is a harried chef. Another friend who sings in her church choir may be thrilled at your inviting her to sing at your wedding, but an overbooked, underpaid cousin who's a professional pianist may regard a similar request in a very different light.

These requests should be made only in response to queries about gifts. If you're in any doubt about the reaction, phrase your request as tentatively as possible to give an out where one might be needed. "Jim and I were wondering how you'd feel about taking the wedding pictures" is a tactfully worded request to a photography buff friend who's just asked what you'd like in the way of a wedding gift. If you can add something about how that friend's style of candid shots perfectly suits the look you want your wedding album to have, so much the better. The request should have as personal a flavor as the gift of time and talent you are soliciting.

Alternatives to Gifts

Should you still have your doubts as to whether or not *any* gift is appropriate, remember that if a wedding is appropriate, so are gifts. Some women getting married for the second or third time to men with a similarly complex marital history feel guilty about getting still another group of presents. One such woman knew she would receive gifts from those few close friends invited to her wedding, but didn't feel she should accept gifts from friends and relatives to whom she simply sent nuptial announcements. Her solution was to have printed at the bottom of the announcement, *No Gifts, Please.*

There are many who would take exception to this way of handling the situation. "No one receiving an announcement without an invitation is obliged to buy a gift, and most don't for a wedding which isn't a first for either bride or groom," says one socially savvy San Francisco woman, "but anyone who wishes to should not be denied the option."

If you agree but still can't bear to think of your sweet and unsophisticated great-aunt Harriet sending you a *third* crystal bowl, you could call her as well as sending the announcement and make your feelings clear. Perhaps you could mention how much your children enjoyed the homemade fudge she sent at Christmas, thus giving her the chance to send *something* if it makes her feel better to do so.

One couple—the groom embarking on his fourth marriage, the bride on her third—found an unusual way around the wedding gift issue. They are both extremely affluent, and they felt awkward about receiving gifts when they already had more than they could possibly fit into the house they were moving to. Yet they were planning a large wedding because they wanted to share the happiness they had found in each other with their many friends, relatives, and business associates. To stem the flow of unwanted gifts and make a meaningful gesture, they wrote a rather lengthy invitation which included the following:

> *Because we met through our volunteer work in the fund-raising activities of the American Cancer Society, because we are so grateful for our health and happiness and so acutely aware of how badly in need of funds the Society is, we are requesting that in lieu of wedding gifts, donations be sent to that worthy organization.*

Of course, such requests are traditionally made only in lieu of flowers being sent to a funeral, so it was an extremely unconventional gesture for a betrothed couple. But this couple felt their request was appropriate, and would be understood by their wedding guests. Another couple met through a hiking and conservation organization about whose work they wanted to educate their friends. In this situation, their request for donations to the organization was adroitly and sincerely worded, and deemed appropriate. Requests like these should always be specific and pertinent, and never made in a casual and perfunctory manner.

The rule of thumb regarding gifts is a simple one: If you don't want many wedding gifts, have a small wedding. Then make your announcements to those not included on your limited guest list in the form of phone calls, which will be less likely to elicit gifts than printed announcements.

Thank-you Notes

Whether you receive many or few gifts, you will want to acknowledge each and every one with a thank-you note as promptly as possible. You can use your personal stationery, or select blank greeting cards. Cards which display reproductions of famous paintings, available in museum gift shops, also work well for thank-you notes. One newlywed couple used a pop art reproduction of a bride and groom, had it copied on individual cards, and wrote their notes on the back. You might also decide to take a photograph from the wedding, make it into a postcard, and use that.

Thank-you notes can help let everyone know your choice for a name if you use stationery imprinted with the name by which you will be known. You might want to have notes printed up with Mrs. Jennifer Winston (your second husband's name), and then underneath write your professional name enclosed in parentheses (Ms. Jennifer Evans).

When it comes to sending thank-you notes, ask your husband if he'd like to write some himself on his personal stationery. You don't have to divvy up the note writing according to whose friends and relatives gave the presents. It's perfectly permissible to reverse the order. In this way you can reach out to people close to him with your offer of friendship and he can do the same with those who are important in your life. Even when you're writing to people you have never met to thank them for a gift as impersonal as cash, you can convey warm and friendly feelings by the tone of the note you send. Here's what one bride wrote to cousins of the groom:

> *Thanks ever so much for the generous check. Tom and I dream of owning a country house, and this will go into our special savings account for that purpose. We'd like to find a place upstate, near the mountains, since we both enjoy fishing and gardening. Perhaps by the next time you come East on a visit, we'll have our dream house and can entertain you there. I do so look forward to meeting you.*

Because you want to send out notes which are sincere, don't fall into the trap of saying how "we'd love for you to come to dinner as soon as we get back from the honeymoon so that you can see for yourselves how lovely the crystal bowl looks on our dining room table," unless you intend to make such an invitation. Such perfunctory phrases are frequently used by first-time brides, but you can find enough honest things to say without making promises you won't be able to keep. The more personalized your thank-you notes, the more they'll reflect the real you.

CHAPTER ELEVEN

Liberated Grooms

First weddings are traditionally the province of the bride. Your second one belongs as much to your groom as to you. Because men and women often have different experiences and expectations about weddings, you should be aware that your fiancé may not perceive these nuptials just the way you do. Talking with prospective and recent grooms provides an insight into the second wedding from the male vantage point. Some of the following comments may shed a new light on your man's attitudes, on his enthusiasms and hesitations about your evolving wedding plans. At the very least, these masculine observations offer you food for thought to be carefully digested.

Robert, a thirty-one-year-old software sales rep, who recently married a divorced woman with a young child, said, "I'm very very much in love with Laura, so when I asked her to marry me, I somehow was picturing her walking down the aisle toward me in a long white veil in a church filled with flowers and the sound of the organ playing the 'Wedding March.' But Laura felt the kind of wedding I was imagining wasn't appropriate for a woman who has already been married and has a child. She wanted us to go off to City Hall and get married quietly, with as little 'fuss' as possible and then leave for a honeymoon. But since this was the only wedding I ever intended to have, I wanted it to be something special. I felt she was cheating me out of the joyful event a wedding should be because of a past that had nothing to do with us.

"My resentment erupted and brought out a lot of problems Laura and I had avoided facing. We went to a couples counselor who specialized in crisis intervention, and we took a serious look at some of the issues the disagreement over the wedding represented. In the presence of the counselor we were able to more fully understand our feelings. I had to accept that I could never be Laura's first husband, and she had to realize that our wedding deserved as much of her energy as her first one had. The wedding we planned started out as a compromise in the counselor's office, but it grew into something that strengthened the mutual understanding between us.

"We were married by a minister on the lawn of the home of the couple who introduced us, surrounded by our families and friends, with Laura's little boy standing next to her throughout the ceremony. Laura didn't wear a white veil but she did wear a lace dress, and the reception turned out to be a wonderful party. *Then* we went on the honeymoon."

"I have three older sisters and each of them had a basic big, showy wedding," said Jonathan, another first-time groom of a second-time bride. A free-lance commercial artist in his late twenties, Jonathan was relieved from the beginning that their wedding wouldn't be a lavish, traditional affair.

"My mom planned all three weddings, and the men my sisters married sat on the sidelines, doing as they were told. The only fun the grooms seemed to have was at their bachelor parties. Because the woman I'm marrying has been married before, she learned enough from experience to leave her mother out of the wedding arrangements and bring me into them. I didn't want us to have a tradition-laden ceremony that in no way reflected our values or the style in which we live our lives. That's why I was so relieved that Alissa shared my views on this subject.

"Our wedding was held in the loft which is my studio and I had painted a huge mural on the walls which celebrated the love we have for each other. Alissa's dress was made by my sister, who's an up-and-coming fashion designer, and the ceremony was performed by a judge who went to college with my uncle. The reception buffet was catered by good friends who own a restaurant and the music was provided by Alissa's best friend's brother's band. It was *our* wedding from start to finish, and it was the best day of both our lives."

Unlike Robert and Jonathan, who had never been married before, Tony brought to his wedding to a second-time bride the hard-won knowledge from his own first marriage. At thirty-seven, Tony is a dedicated physician who talked frankly and thoughtfully about the differences in his two weddings.

"I think my first marriage started to fall apart at the wedding. I come from a large, close-knit, highly emotional Italian-American family. My first wife's parents are very suburban, and very concerned about doing things the correct way. And that's the kind of wedding we had, from the church service to the country club reception. My family, particularly my mother, felt excluded, snubbed in dozens of hurtful little ways. I realize now that I should have stepped in and been more protective of my family, but I was in the first year of my residency and too immersed in work to think about much else. I left the wedding plans entirely to my fiancée and her mother, and the result was an occasion in which my family had no part.

"That clash of styles and a reluctance to compromise on both our parts cropped up again and again in the three years Audrey and I were married. It was when we started talking about having a baby that we both realized we couldn't imagine spending the rest of our lives together. The divorce was brisk, amicable, and efficient. And it left me feeling absolutely empty inside with nothing but my work to give meaning to my life.

"Then I met Maggie. Like me, she comes from a big family, Irish in her case. Because she works in a hospital, she can understand a lot more about the pressures I'm under than Audrey could. Maggie has three children from her first marriage, which ended in a messy divorce. She would have liked a religious wedding but couldn't have one because she is divorced from a man she married in the Church. We were married on the front porch of Maggie's sister's house, with a local justice of the peace officiating. We wrote our own service and exchanged vows which included religious sentiments. I know that the ceremony was very meaningful to everyone there."

The reception was held on the patio of the bride's sister's house. The groom's mother and aunts brought heaping platters of homemade lasagna, huge bowls of meatballs, and a wedding cake from an Italian bakery. The bride's mother had made corned beef, and her sister's husband brought a keg of beer. The band played Irish jigs and Italian folk dances.

"Both families felt at home during the wedding, and Maggie's children were very much a part of the celebration. Maggie and I are committed to each other and I felt the wedding we had conveyed that commitment to all the people who are important to us. And that, to me, is what a wedding is all about," Tony happily concluded.

A second marriage for a widower carries a set of emotions different from that of a man whose first marriage ended in divorce. Frederik, a sixty-six-year-old retired corporate executive, recently married a woman his own age. Like Frederik, Sylvia had been widowed a few years earlier.

"Planning the wedding was a bit painful, I have to admit. I know Sylvia felt the same way. When we each married the first time, back in our early twenties, we thought of it as being for life, and never envisioned the possibility of another wedding. When my wife died, I couldn't imagine remarrying, nor could

Sylvia when she lost her husband. But when we got to know each other and realized we wanted to spend what's left of our lives together, we decided to marry. We didn't want to be married in church because there were too many associations from our first weddings. But we are both religious and we wanted our second wedding to be sanctified by God, so we married in our minister's study, which united us in the eyes of God without standing up at the altar. Only our children and their spouses were with us for the ceremony.

"Then Sylvia's daughter threw us a party with lots of family, a few old friends, and an old-fashioned wedding luncheon. The grandchildren on both sides were all there, so it was quite a party. Sylvia and I know we can't be young again and this wedding wasn't what the first one was, but just the fact that we found each other and are building a new life is something of a miracle."

A widower in his early forties, Alex, the owner of a construction company and the father of four, lost his wife to an automobile accident two years before he married Marilyn, the divorced mother of three children ranging in age from fourteen to six.

"Marilyn's only hesitation about marrying me was that it was too soon after Rochelle's death. Maybe it was, but I knew Marilyn was the woman I wanted to continue my life with because she had brought me hope when I was in the midst of despair. Meanwhile, I was still dealing with very painful memories while we were planning the wedding. And Marilyn had her own problems about the past to contend with. Her husband had left her for another woman when she was pregnant with her youngest child. It's taken her six years to get over the bitterness. I think the only reason she reached out to me was that my grief made me a less threatening figure than a divorced man who'd been on the singles scene for a while.

"Marilyn and I decided we didn't want a church wedding. I haven't practiced my religion since my wife's death, and Marilyn's been pretty lax about hers since the divorce. We didn't want to be hypocrites. What we did want was a wedding which would symbolize the new life we were determined to build from the wreckage of our old ones. The summer after my wife's death, I took up sailing as a distraction and really got into it. Since I hadn't gone sailing during my first marriage, there were no memories to mar my enjoyment of it. I met Marilyn at the sailing club, and the sport was the first bond between us. That's why we decided to have a wedding reception involving sailboats."

Marilyn and Alex were married in the Town Hall with all seven children surrounding them. Afterward, the whole family boarded the forty-foot schooner the bride and groom had given each other for a wedding present. Fellow members of the sailing club took their boats out at the same time, forming a nuptial regalia as they all sailed to a cove. There they dropped anchor, waded ashore, built a fire, and had a clambake. A performer hired for the occasion entertained everyone singing sea chanteys while playing an accordion. As dusk fell, bottles of champagne and a wedding cake with white icing and light blue trimmings were produced from coolers, and everyone toasted the bride and groom.

"Friends took our kids back to shore while Marilyn and I spent the first night of our married life sleeping on the deck of our very own boat." Alex's face broke into a grin when recalling this romantic conclusion to his nuptial tale.

Planning a wedding which would help cement a new family was very much on the mind of Barry, a twenty-eight-year-old sales manager and first-time groom, who married a widow eight years older than himself, the mother of two teenage children.

"I didn't want a big, fancy wedding because it's not my style, nor is it June's. She had that kind of wedding the first time and wouldn't consider doing it again. June's husband died of cancer almost four years ago. We met through a mountain climbing club we both belong to. With June there were none of the quarrels I was used to with my former girlfriend. We got along wonderfully well from the start, but her kids found it difficult to accept me.

"The most successful times I had with the kids were when we all went backpacking together. June had always taken them on her mountain climbing trips, so it was an activity they associated with her, but not with their father. It was on the trails that they treated me most like a father. When June and I first talked about getting married and she expressed her worries about her children's reaction to it, she said as a joke that they'd probably like it best if we got married on a mountaintop.

"Well, that's just what we did. We went on a fairly strenuous full-day's climb with June's kids, and a bunch of our friends who are backpackers, and their kids. One of the men is a minister and he married us on a windy mountaintop at sunset. After setting up camp we had a cookout supper, then we danced around the campfire before turning in for the night. The next day when we began the descent from the campsite, I had the feeling that we were coming down from the mountain different than we had come up it. We were now a real family."

"Jill's friends all tell her that she's taking quite a chance with a three-time loser like me but we're both convinced that this time it will be different," said Mark, a thrice-married man in his mid-forties. "I was too young for my first marriage, too obsessed with business in my second, and in my third there was an essential emotional incompatibility. With Jill, it all clicks. She was married once before, when she was in college, and divorced before she graduated. Jill is twelve years younger than I am, but her values are very solid. She didn't have any children in her first marriage and we plan to start a family shortly after we're married. I have two daughters from my second marriage and a son from my third, but I never spent enough time with them when they were little. That's something else which will be different this time," Mark said resolutely.

Mark and Jill see their wedding as the first test of his determination to be more involved in their marriage than he was in his three previous ones.

"Jill never had a real wedding and she always dreamed of one," Mark explained. His own first wedding was traditional, the second was in the middle of a Hawaiian honeymoon, and the third was a casual brunch. "I didn't particularly want a lavish wedding for my fourth marriage, but I knew how important having one was to Jill, so I agreed to go along with it," Mark said.

The only problem was that Jill wanted more from him than just going along with it. She insisted that Mark join her in every aspect of the planning for the wedding.

"The wedding is set for next month, and I'm getting into the swing of things more than I would have thought possible. I've gone to caterers and travel agents, picked out stationery for announcements and invitations, planned the menu for the wedding rehearsal dinner, and written thank-you notes for some of the presents which have already arrived. The more I do, the more committed I feel to this wedding and, consequently, to the marriage. Now even our most skeptical friends are beginning to believe I'm a changed man."

Whether or not Mark is really a changed man remains to be seen, but no one can deny that he and Jill are getting off to a good start. So can you and your groom, regardless of past histories. Think of this wedding not as a prelude to your marriage but as the first stage of it. The ways in which you communicate feelings, work out differences, and join forces for a common goal are significant far beyond this brief nuptial period. Keep in mind that the man you're marrying has his own disquieting memories, spurts of anxiety, and far-reaching hopes just as you do. Share all your anticipations and apprehensions with him, and get him to share his with you. It's the best way of making this wedding a solid foundation on which to build your forthcoming marriage.

CHAPTER TWELVE

Prenuptial Agreements

"Three weeks before marrying a man I adored, he was asking me to sign a paper concerning what I would and would not be entitled to in the event of our divorce!" Irene's voice quivered with incredulity at the recollection, even though the experience she was describing had occurred two years earlier. Irene was a high school math teacher, whose first husband was an aspiring actor making a scanty living at a variety of jobs. When the marriage ended in a no-fault divorce, they each went their separate ways, nursing emotional wounds but unconcerned about financial settlements because there weren't any finances to settle. A few years later, Irene met Arnold, a man twelve years older than she, who had gotten divorced about the same time she had. But Arnold's marriage had lasted for almost twenty years, had produced three children, and there were considerable financial assets involved in the divorce.

"Arnold felt he got a bad deal in the family courts over the settlement awarded to his first wife," Irene said. "He told me that at the time of his divorce, he made a promise to himself that he would never marry again without a prenuptial agreement clearly defining what his wife would be entitled to should that marriage also end in divorce."

When Arnold first mentioned the agreement to Irene, they were already engaged, and she was astonished that the subject was even coming up. "To me prenuptial agreements were for Jackie Kennedy and Aristotle Onassis, or big-time rock stars, movie moguls, people like that. I couldn't see what they could have to do with me."

Along with her amazement, Irene was enraged. "Here I was marrying a man I loved, respected, and admired, and he was acting like I was a gold digger from whom he had to protect himself. If it weren't so insulting, I would have found it ludicrous."

When Irene indignantly said she would have nothing to do with such an odious idea, Arnold said he didn't feel comfortable getting married without it. Irene replied that she didn't feel comfortable getting married *with* it. They ended up seeing a couples therapist, and in the neutral environment of the therapist's office, Irene was able to understand just how scarred by the circumstances of his divorce Arnold was, how much anger he still held toward his ex-wife. He, in turn, calmed down enough to take a look at the situation from Irene's point of view. In the end, she did sign the agreement and they did get married, but Irene's hurt lingered long after the ink was dry on the agreement, which took away her right to any substantial settlement from Arnold, should either of them ever seek a divorce.

Although her marriage is, so far, a success, Irene remains resentful about the agreement. "It's called a prenuptial, or antenuptial, agreement, but I think of it as an antinuptial agreement," Irene quipped bitterly about the document which almost ended her second marriage before it began.

There are two arguments on this prickly topic of prenuptial agreements. The romantic one is that a marriage should be based on love and trust, and if this is absent from the beginning, why bother to marry? The other point of view is more pragmatic. Marriage, it argues, is as much a social contract as a personal one. It must conform to the laws of the state in which it is being performed, whether or not it is sanctioned by a religious authority. Since it is an official, public act, and not simply an emotional and private bonding, there is no reason why an additional legal document shouldn't be added into the marriage procedure. Which side you take in this debate will depend on both your personal values and histories.

Usually, prenuptial agreements are required of a future second wife by men who feel they were taken advantage of financially by a first wife. But as more women are earning high salaries and acquiring substantial monetary assets, they, too, are seriously considering demanding prenuptial agreements, particularly in second marriages. Sandy was one such woman. An MBA earning a substantial six-figure income, she made some very shrewd investments and owned property of considerable value. Sandy and her ex-husband, also a success in the business world, went through exhausting hassles about property division during their divorce. Her second marriage was to a publicist who worked for a nonprofit organization. She sincerely admired her fiancé's idealism, but couldn't ignore the discrepancies in their incomes. In their case, the woman asked for the prenuptial agreement and the man's feelings were hurt by the request.

Sandy's fiancé, Roger, wanted her to put off the agreement till after the wedding. "I guess I can understand her wanting to protect herself, given the fact that half of American marriages end in divorce," Roger glumly conceded, but he added that he didn't want their "prenuptial joy shattered by the pain this prenuptial agreement was causing me."

While she felt sympathy for Roger's point of view, Sandy had her own questions about turning a prenuptial agreement into a postnuptial one. "Obviously, I would never have married a man I thought I couldn't trust to sign it afterward," she hastened to explain. "It was just that," she continued with a frown, "it went against my business instincts to put off signing a contract until after the logical time to sign it had passed."

Sandy finally decided to turn the prenuptial agreement into a postnuptial one in order to spare her fiancé's feelings and to demonstrate her trust in him. But the clash of viewpoints between her and Roger typifies the differences in thinking between those people who are and are not business-oriented. One groom refused his fiancée's request to wait till after the wedding before signing the agreement, which severely limited her rights to any of his property in any subsequent divorce action.

"It's not that I don't trust Sharon not to sign it," Al said tensely. "But what's the point of it if it's not signed *before* the marriage?"

"What's the point of getting married if first I have to sign a document which makes a mockery of all the marriage vows?" Sharon angrily retorted.

Sharon and Al postponed their wedding till they could work out this thorny problem but she went along with his wishes in the end. "I don't think I would have signed it if I hadn't been married before. But since I knew from my personal experience how a marriage could fall apart, I was better able to understand Al's viewpoint, no matter how much it hurt me," she said thoughtfully.

Since it's usually the woman being asked to sign a prenuptial agreement, if she has been through a marriage and divorce, she's more likely to understand a request a first-time bride might see as degrading.

It's a delicate balance, this dangling between romance and realism, between hope born afresh with a new commitment and the cynicism which lingers after a disillusioning experience. The whole issue is made easier when the prospective bride and groom both have sufficiently substantial assets to make such an agreement seem reasonable all around. Even when this isn't the case, the way the question is raised, from the phrasing to the timing, can make it easier on the less-affluent partner.

If there are children involved, the advisability of prenuptial agreements becomes more obviously apparent. A spouse is automatically entitled to inherit a specified portion of a deceased person's estate, the amount varying from state to state. Therefore, if a man or woman wants his or her children to inherit the bulk of an estate rather than someone to whom they may have been married for a very short time, a prenuptial agreement is the way to ensure this. The will should then be changed to correspond to the prenuptial agreement, but without the spouse's agreeing to be excluded from the bulk of the inheritance, a change in the will has no effect.

So emotionally charged is the subject of premarital agreements that many lawyers don't recommend them unless there is a substantial inheritance to safeguard for children of a former marriage. "I would never suggest it for any other reason," said Manhattan attorney Sidney Strauss. "If a couple broaches the subject to me, I simply explain to them what such an agreement entails. When I first started my practice, no one asked about prenuptial agreements, but now as divorce settlements become more complex, questions about these agreements become more common."

Many New York matrimonial attorneys are observing not only the proliferation of these agreements but their adoption as a kind of "blueprint for marital behavior," according to a trendy Manhattan magazine. Some couples are writing into the agreement absurd stipulations, such as limiting the amount of weight a spouse may gain or agreeing on specifics of future children's education.

Now that prenuptial agreements are so popular, they are also more frequently contested. Disputed prenuptial agreements now comprise a significant segment of matrimonial legal practice in New York. While many attorneys handling these agreements view them as a sensible procedure for protecting assets, marriage counselors see them as blueprints for divorce because they undermine the sense of commitment essential to a successful marriage. Whether prenuptial agreements reflect the current high rate of marital failure or are contributing to it is an issue open to debate. But it behooves any couple entering a marriage where at least one party has substantial assets to be informed of the particulars of the prenuptial option.

The complexities of divorce law vary from state to state. In California, with its famous community property law, prenuptial agreements are used more often than anywhere else. All properties are divided fifty-fifty in California unless a prenuptial agreement predetermines another proportion of distribution. This type of agreement can also be a wise precaution in a state such as New York, where the outcome of divorce settlements is very much up for grabs. New York has a system called "equitable distribution." This means that if a couple can't come to terms themselves about a property settlement, it is determined by the court, which must make its decision based upon ten criteria set forth in the law.

The first nine criteria range from the length of the marriage to the employment situation of both parties. The last criterion is anything else the judge deems to be of significance. It is this vague wording, so open to the subjective evaluation of any judge, which makes the more affluent partner, usually the man, wary of leaving the distribution of his property to the courts in the eventuality of an acrimonious divorce. And it is the anticipation of divorce which insults, enrages, and humiliates the other party, usually the woman.

While you might like to close your eyes and return to that rapturous moment when the two of you made a commitment to get married, the subject of prenuptial agreements, once mentioned by either party, won't go away, but must be dealt with maturely and rationally. Here are some suggestions for dealing with this unpleasant, but sometimes unavoidable, issue:

1. If you are remarrying and have both children and assets, whether they be a house, savings, or investments, you should bring up the possibility of a prenuptial agreement. The two of you can talk it over between yourselves and see if it makes sense. Try to keep this conversation responsible, realistic, and reasonable. If protection of your children is the primary rationale for a prenuptial agreement, it's usually possible to keep emotional reactions to a minimum.

2. If you have no children but do have substantial assets, you may still want to raise this topic. Prepare to deal with some outraged feelings on the part of your fiancé, particularly if his own financial picture is less rosy than yours. In this case, try to stay firm and calm. Do not become defensive. Point out that you have already had at least one marriage which didn't work out. If he has had one too, your point will hit home more effectively. If it is you who is the only one with a previously failed marriage as well as more assets, tact and kindness will be called for. But don't placate or equivocate.

If this agreement makes sense to you, your opinion shouldn't be swayed by protestations of good intentions because you know they're there or you wouldn't be marrying him. Simply say that in view of your own marital track record and the national statistics, plus the problems of divorce settlements particular to whatever state you live in, you would feel more comfortable with this agreement.

3. Should your fiancé become impatient and impulsively offer simply to sign and forget this troublesome document, tell him that he should consult an attorney of his own. Explain that no one should sign a legal document without counsel.

4. If you are the one being asked to sign such an agreement, first ascertain your fiancé's precise reasons for requiring your signature on this document. If you are outraged at the

lack of trust, you should let him know this because unexpressed feelings will crop up later to haunt the relationship. But you should always be willing to hear—and try to understand—his point of view. Listen to what he is saying in the context of his own marital history, and the broader social climate of unstable marriages and lengthy court battles. Don't try to dissuade him from asking you for something which is obviously very important to him. Assurances of your integrity are not the issue here. You are probably dealing with a promise he made to himself before he even met you and to which he feels committed to standing firm.

5. Tell him that you must get an impartial expert to look over the document before you sign it. If you already have a lawyer, consult with him or her. If not, find one. Do *not* let your fiancé talk you into consulting his lawyer. This agreement is predicated on a business basis, and it's never good business to enter into a contractual agreement without independent legal advice.

6. When you see a lawyer, make certain that you fully comprehend his explanation of the implications of what you are signing. Be prepared for him to ask you if, in your opinion, this agreement gives a full disclosure of your fiancé's assets. Also be ready to discuss the possibility of a termination clause being written into the document. This means that if you are still married at the expiration of a specified amount of time, the document is null and void.

If your fiancé is reluctant to insert such a clause, ascertain the reasons for his reluctance. If they make sense to you, fine. If not, you two have a lot more talking to do before you see your respective lawyers again.

7. If you are unable to agree on certain specifics of the prenuptial agreement, a lot of bitter feelings may be stirred up. At this point, it's preferable to consult a couples therapist

before you both have lawyers verbally slugging it out. If you can't work through this misunderstanding before the marriage, you might have to postpone the wedding until you can.

8. If, as in the great majority of the cases, the prenuptial agreement is signed to mutual satisfaction, then put it out of your mind. Forget the business of legal documents and return to the joy of your prenuptial plans, where the only agreement is to make each other superbly happy for the rest of your lives.

CHAPTER THIRTEEN

Prenuptial Romance

Although the weeks and months before your wedding may be tense, as the endless planning clashes with demands of jobs and children, it is important not to lose sight of the romance which caused all these preparations in the first place. Be sure to set some evenings aside for just the two of you to get away from the checklists and schedules and constant arrangements. Savor each other's company, whether it be for a candlelight dinner, a drive in the country, a walk through the city, or whatever you both find relaxing, romantic, and private.

As the weeks approaching the wedding fly by, you will feel more pressure on you. If you have opted to go on a honeymoon immediately after the wedding, then you will be planning a vacation as well as a wedding. When there are children involved, especially two sets, they may increase their demands for your free time as the big day approaches. Trying to take care of dozens of practical matters, go to work every day, and still be sensitive to the emotional needs of your children can take its toll on your relationship. Even if it's not September, the days may dwindle down to a precious few, and those few days will be increasingly difficult to spend together.

A good way to steal some spare time is for both of you to arrange a day off from work. Now, with the kids in school and the pressures of the workplace on hold for one precious day, you can accomplish some necessary tasks and give yourselves a romantic day all at once. Perhaps begin with a breakfast of coffee and croissants at a local patisserie. Then take care of doctors' appointments for blood tests if you live in a state which requires them, or apply for your marriage license.

Or take time for a leisurely lunch at a restaurant which has special associations for you or an ambience conducive to an amorous mood. Lingering over your meal, you can talk about the wedding rings you will be selecting in the afternoon. These rings, which will be the visible symbol of your union, deserve your most romantic feelings for their contemplation. Of course, you will have discussed the matter before, but now would be a fitting moment to talk over ideas for engraving them.

Many couples engrave only their names and the date of the wedding. You might, however, have a special pet phrase, acronym, or term of endearment and choose that instead. The language of love two people share at their most affectionate moments is unique to them. A phrase from a poem or prayer you both cherish can also be written inside your rings and serve as a bond between you. Remember that both rings don't have to carry identical phrases, though most couples prefer that they do; each ring should express the deepest feelings you have for your beloved.

Unlike the engagement ring, which is often far less important in a second marriage, the wedding ring remains an essential component of the wedding ceremony. Some women who wore a plain gold band during their first marriage want a different kind of ring for the second. If you don't have an engagement ring this time, you might opt for a more expensive band set with precious stones for your wedding. Keep in mind that diamonds are the most enduring of stones, certain to stand the test of time, and can be worn constantly. Rubies, emeralds, and sapphires are softer stones and can crack or scratch if they are worn every day.

Certain religious considerations come into the selection of the ring. In the Jewish faith, for instance, the wedding ring must be a smooth circle, unbroken by any ornaments or stones. When a plain gold band is your choice, for whatever reason, you might like an antique ring, or you may want to design your own and have your jeweler make it up for you. One second bride used her grandmother's ring at the marriage ceremony, but afterward wore a diamond band she and her husband picked out together.

In the jewelry store, select your rings carefully. Make sure the style, size, and shape are just what you want. Try on several rings, and slip them on each other's finger to get the feel of them. Only when you are absolutely certain that these are the rings you want on your fingers for the rest of your lives should you finalize the purchase and order the engraving.

While double-ring ceremonies are widespread, grooms at second weddings choose to wear a ring more often than those at first-time weddings. Experience teaches the value of symbols of commitment, and more mature men have learned this lesson. A double-ring ceremony also fits the mood of mutuality and equality which you want in your second marriage. If your first wedding involved only one ring, you have a new and wonderful experience to look forward to—placing the pledge of your devotion on your husband's finger. If you are already wearing an engagement ring, remember to transfer it to the fourth finger of your right hand before the ceremony so that your groom slips the wedding ring on a bare fourth finger of the left hand.

It's up to you to see that the mood of this romantic interlude lingers in the frenetic days ahead. Remember, you want to be a radiant bride, not a frazzled juggler of time for fiancé, children, and job. Retaining a romantic aura will ensure that radiance triumphs when you want it the most. If you are keeping a journal of this prenuptial period, make an entry about how you felt on your romantic day off, so that you can refer to it when you feel the tedium of everyday life dragging you down from the romantic high.

If you're not keeping such a journal, you might think about starting one. It's a good way to keep track of your impressions and emotions as your wedding approaches. If the idea of writing entries in a notebook strikes you as just one more grinding task, consider the alternative of a cassette tape recorder. You could try talking your feelings into it, thus creating a high-tech prenuptial diary.

Look at this period as a trial run for the marriage it precedes. Develop productive habits of communication with your future husband *now*. Don't harbor grievances, thinking that this harried period isn't the time to air them. If you don't express your annoyances and resentments now, they will fester and burst out in destructive ways later. Remember that your marriage will be full of pressures and that you will often feel pulled in several directions at once. The wedding period may intensify these feelings but they won't disappear once you are married. The more directly you deal with them now, the less likely they will be to haunt you later.

Promise yourself to take the following precautions against letting the daily hassles erode the romantic feelings:

1. **Talk** to Each Other

When something's bothering you, *tell* him; when you sense he's troubled about something, *ask* him what's on his mind. As you thrash out differing preferences about particular aspects of the wedding, keep an open mind. Ask yourself if it's really your fiancé you're angry with, or an interfering member of his family. Perhaps you're more affected by the resentment of his children than you realize and you're taking it out on their father. When you find yourself reacting defensively to disagreements with him about the role of your children in the wedding, examine your own emotions before attacking his point of view.

Don't let shadows come between you. If you feel your fiancé is bringing experiences from his first wedding into the plans for this second one, gently point out to him that history is not going to repeat itself. When you find irrational reactions on your part, eruptions of anger, a rush of bitter feelings which you can't account for, think carefully about their source. They may lie in unresolved feelings about your first marriage. Make it a point to share these insights with your fiancé. Don't ever forget that the only way to banish emotional ghosts is to openly confront them by talking about them with the person closest to you.

Lay down some ground rules for quarrels right now. First of all, don't be afraid of quarrels. Handled with finesse, they can clear the air rather than pile up resentments. Probably more resentments build up from quarrels which are suppressed than from those which bubble up to the surface. When there's an issue over the wedding plans about which the two of you disagree, take a long look at it. It's a bit like an archeology dig, because as you burrow beneath the surface clash of views, you'll find emotional debris from previous marriages and love affairs. Sort it all through together. Then deal with the issue at hand. Suddenly, it may not seem all that irreconcilable.

2. *Take Time Out for* **You**

The two of you, that is. It's a strange period, this prenuptial one, no longer a courtship, not yet a marriage. Keep doing the things which brought you together in the first place. Play tennis, go to the theater, or talk about sports, politics, or literature—whatever you did before. Don't limit all your conversations to wedding plans, nor all your activities to chores associated with them. Continue to do what you've always enjoyed sharing together instead of delaying all leisure time pursuits till after the wedding. Don't let this prenuptial time be full of tensions and dissent. Let it prefigure the good times your marriage will bring to both of you.

3. *Let the Romance Thrive*

Romance too often gets lost in the prenuptial rush. Don't let this happen to you. Think up more treats for the two of you, like the day you took off to buy the wedding rings and apply for your marriage license. Continue to give each other little impromptu presents, plan the kind of surprises you did before you became engaged. Don't ever get so harried with wedding plans that you stop feeling sexy, or letting him know you find him so. The smart woman is aware of the fact that many men fear romance ends at the altar. Don't let your fiancé wonder if, perhaps, it hasn't ended even sooner. It's a mistake to work so strenuously on the wedding plans that you forget how to play, how to be carefree, soft, and seductive.

Remember that this wedding is the *result* of a romance. Feelings of romance between you are at the core of your commitment to each other. If you're going to keep these fires of passion burning during your marriage despite the demands of daily life, don't do any less in these weeks prior to the marriage. Of course, there are real time pressures as the wedding day approaches, but never lose sight of the romance which started it all. Whatever drew you to each other strongly enough to decide on this marriage should not be forgotten in the frenetic time of wedding preparations. Keep your priorities straight, and your prenuptial period will set the tone for the romance-filled marriage which awaits you.

CHAPTER FOURTEEN

Radiance Redux

Back in the social Dark Ages before people learned that cere-monies were made for them rather than they for ceremonies, the color of a bride's attire was rigidly proscribed. White was expected of first-time brides—whose virginity was presumed. Second-time brides wore off-white or dove gray or pale mauve as befitted their halfway status.

But since virginity is no longer an assumption for first-time brides, the question of wearing white loses some of its impact. And what of the second-time bride who yearns for that white wedding dress she never wore? By all means, wear it, provided you can pull it off—meaning you're still fairly young, and your first marriage produced no children. If you eloped when you were eighteen, and now, at twenty-one, you're about to marry again, a white wedding gown is perfectly appropriate. If, how-ever, your first wedding was a large, formal event, and you won't see twenty-anything again, think twice about wearing white, even if you have no children. There are subtle questions of taste and sentiment here which bear careful scrutiny.

One arbiter of good taste and rarified sensibility, who fully agrees with the eschewing of white, is the incomparable Miss

Manners, who provides the following words of wisdom on the subject in her *Guide to Excruciatingly Correct Behavior:*

> *The effect of the white dress should be fresh and sweet—an effect that is not usually what women who are older and wiser want to project. The difference is what makes people cry at first weddings, and smile at subsequent ones, smiles being infinitely more complicated than tears.*

In these complicated days, even first-time brides don't necessarily wear white unless they are opting for a conventional processional, replete with veil, train, and all the other traditional trimmings.

"I didn't even wear white the *first* time," exclaimed Carla, a public relations consultant. After living with her first husband for nearly five years before their marriage, Carla said she would have felt "like a hypocrite" had she worn pristine white to her wedding, which was full of people who had been guests at the couple's jointly owned summer home.

"Since I wore a long-waisted, champagne-colored crepe silk dress for my first wedding, I wondered what I was going to do for an encore," Carla recalled as she talked about her second wedding. Deciding to listen to the dictates of personal taste, rather than to an antiquated dress code, Carla wore red for her second wedding, which took place at Christmastime. She wondered, however, whether she was flouting convention a little too much.

Nervously consulting a friend who was the fashion editor of a small weekly newspaper, Carla was warmly reassured that her choice was perfectly acceptable. Her friend told Carla that her vibrant red wool suit was both appropriate to the holiday season and suitable to her personal style, which has always been somewhat flamboyant. Carla wore a headpiece of lush white orchids, dainty white gloves, and a corsage of more white orchids at her waist, as well as white faille pumps. The hotel dining room where the fashionable wedding brunch was held was decorated in Christmas colors, which were wonderfully highlighted by the bride's dashing red suit and soft white flowers.

Bright colors *are* appropriate for a second-time bride. If your favorite color is turquoise, there's no reason why you can't wear a suit in that color. You can choose any number of materials, from wool or crepe de chine in winter, to linen or a light silk in warmer weather. White flowers and white pearls will give a softening tone, a radiantly bridal cast to a suit whose color is not a conventionally nuptial one. Silk faille pumps, silk stockings, and flowers in the hair, at the bosom, or at the waist all serve to add a bridal touch to the most strikingly shaded outfits. Think about hot pinks, bright yellows, and deep greens. Stay away from mauve or gray—you're the bride, not her mother. If a cream-colored silk or linen suit feels right to you, by all means wear it, but there is absolutely no reason for you to feel limited to any of the off-white variants. Remember that this is *your* day; vibrant, hot colors will make you stand out from the crowd.

Second-time brides, being more practical than their first-time counterparts, often want a dress they can wear again. The savvy shopper buying her second-wedding outfit usually steers clear of the bridal boutiques of big department stores, preferring to search in the evening wear sections of these stores. A simple cocktail dress can look very formal if it has rhinestone buttons. Or consider an elegant two-piece dress with a jacket, which can be removed after the ceremony so that you are festively sleeveless for the reception. An apricot suit might do very nicely if it is of a sufficiently sharp shade for the vibrance you want to convey. Even that old standby, the navy blue suit, can work if it's worn with a frilly white blouse, several ropes of milky pearls, a fluffy, flowery headpiece, and a delicate gardenia corsage.

Harriet Love, the highly innovative owner of a vintage clothing boutique in downtown Manhattan's trendy SoHo art colony, is full of intriguing suggestions for fashion-conscious women who want to look stunning at their second wedding:

- A beautiful forties midcalf crepe suit, white with navy trim
- A chiffon pattern from the thirties
- A very sophisticated linen suit
- A brilliantly colored knit suit
- A classic forties or fifties suit designed by Chanel, Scaasi, or any top designer

"Hats," suggests Harriet Love, "make a statement." She says you can find a beautiful old 1915 hat, sew silk flowers on its brim, and tie it with a marvelous piece of tulle for a feminine and old-fashioned effect.

Ms. Love urges second-time brides to show some ingenuity in putting together a dynamic wedding outfit. If you find a blouse, perhaps a beaded crepe, that you're just crazy about but can't find a matching skirt, she suggests looking around in vintage clothing stores till you find one that will go with the blouse.

While she's all for initiative and creativity in the selection of second-wedding attire, Harriet Love also advocates listening to the dictates of common sense and good taste in your choices. Classic suits, not above knee length, are more appropriate for women ages thirty-five to fifty than are antique dresses. These, she maintains, are more suitable to second-time brides in the age bracket of twenty to thirty-five. She also cautions the younger shopper to keep in mind that "antique" doesn't mean shabby, and that the vintage dress of your choice must be in perfect condition to be worn by the contemporary bride.

Late Victorian and early Edwardian dresses, with their mutton sleeves, high collars, and tight waists in cream, buff, or light blue lace, with a train which was popular at the turn of the century, can make perfect wedding dresses. If you want to travel farther back into the Victorian past, you will find dresses with bustles, hoops, or crinolines, one of which may capture your imagination.

For American history buffs, the mid-Victorian flounce connotes the Civil War period. If you have an enterprising dressmaker who could turn you into an antebellum belle for a day, you are all set. There's no reason why fascination with a particular historical period can't determine your choice of attire for this highly individualized second wedding of yours. If you have a passion for the Regency period, you can have an empire-waisted, floor-length dress designed especially for you in materials and colors as varied as maroon velvet or peach muslin.

Your wedding does not have to be a costume ball for you to come dressed in the clothes of another era. One woman, a student of Japanese, married her second husband in an antique kimono. A professor of women's studies wore the high-necked, full-sleeved blouse and long skirt of the Gibson Girl, who characterized the period when women were first fighting for their rights.

With enough daring and imagination, you can dress as any woman who has ever held a fascination for you, from Marie Antoinette to Mary Pickford. Frivolous flapper, prototypical feminist, sizzling siren—you're free to take your pick and bring out whatever aspect of yourself intrigues you the most.

Don't worry about finding complementary costumes for your attendants. There is no reason why you can't mix and match the styles of your bridal party. You can let your maid of honor and bridesmaids wear whatever they like. If a teenaged girl is marching in your procession, a Laura Ashley–type dress is always appropriate. In other words, your outfit can be as costume-like or as flamboyant as you like, and the other women in your wedding party can be more conventionally attired.

But this mixing and matching of styles is good only if you

feel comfortable letting others follow their own preferences. If, on the other hand, you are the type of person who likes to plan the whole show down to every last detail, who wants to orchestrate the entire wedding and control every aspect, then you will want to pick attendants who will go along with your choices. If you've decided to walk down the aisle dressed as a Shakespearean heroine and you want your bridesmaids attired in Elizabethan costume, be sure to pick only attendants who can handle such a theatrical wedding.

Sometimes the theme can be dramatic, but you can still arrange a conservative outfit for your conventionally minded best friend whom you chose to be matron of honor. One widow in her thirties with several children of her own, marrying a man whose two previous marriages had produced five children, got married on Halloween. All the kids and their friends had the time of their lives dressing up as witches, ghosts, and goblins. Although the bride wore an antique orange taffeta dress, her matron of honor still fit the flamboyant theme and was perfectly appropriate in a black lace evening dress. If you are planning an unconventional theme and want your wedding party in complementary costumes, it's only fair to discuss this first with potential attendants to see if they feel comfortable with your plans.

How does your groom fit into your costume plans? This is another of those subjects the two of you will have to discuss thoroughly to make sure you are thinking as one person on the matter. Sometimes a shared interest which includes special attire can provide the theme for the wedding. One couple with a passion for sailing were married on a friend's yacht in matching sailor suits. The bride wore a pleated white skirt and white sailor blouse with light blue trimming, and the groom dressed in white trousers, navy blazer, and striped tie. Another couple, who had met on the bridle path while out riding, were married at the estate of wealthy relatives. The bride wore a nineteenth-century riding habit, and even had an antique sidesaddle brought out to give the guests a demonstration of how ladies of yore "sat" a horse. The groom also wore an elegant riding habit. The wedding was celebrated at a champagne brunch set up under an enormous oak tree on the lawn near the stables.

On the whole, men are more conservative and conventional about clothes than are women. Don't coerce your fiancé into donning duds in which you may find him dashing, but in which he feels foolish in front of family and friends. If he's willing to be Lord Nelson to your Lady Hamilton, or to play Rhett to your Scarlett, consider yourself lucky. But if such carryings-on aren't for your Mr. Right, don't push it. The bride can be a bit outrageous and the groom as straight as an arrow and the wedding will still be a smashing success.

Let your groom decide on the clothes he and his best man and any ushers are going to wear. The groom should be as pleased and comfortable with his attire as you are with yours. Many women who encourage their future second husband to share fully in the wedding plans balk when it comes to fashion, which they consider strictly a feminine province. Don't dictate to your fiancé how he, his brother, and his best friend should dress for what is as much his wedding as yours.

Even the most contemporary second-time bride has trouble letting go of the tradition of not letting the groom see her before the ceremony on her wedding day. Some women like to surprise the man they are marrying by not letting him see their wedding outfit beforehand. If this kind of surprise seems romantic to you, by all means keep your bridal outfit a secret. But such a style doesn't fit every relationship. It hardly applies to the harried female accountant marrying a fashion design student a few years younger than herself who is only too happy to let her wedding dress be his creation. In some cases, you may both enjoy the prospect of shopping for your wedding clothes together.

"My second husband is much more style-conscious than I am," said Barbara, a sports-minded management consultant. "Before we were married, Ron always came with me when I bought clothes. Before I knew him, I hated shopping. But since he is in my life, I adore buying clothes because I can try them on for Ron and get his feedback."

For couples like Barbara and Ron, shopping for her wedding dress can be a highlight of their nuptial preparations. But even for couples where the woman makes all her own fashion decisions, shopping for a wedding dress together can be fun and romantic and bring you closer. If your memory of buying a wedding gown is of a bashful young woman deferentially following her decisive mother into the bridal boutique, this is the time to create an entirely different scenario.

Just close your eyes and picture a couple at any stage of life, very much in love. Now see them strolling hand-in-hand through department stores, vintage clothing stores, costume shops, clever little boutiques, famous fashion emporiums, wherever their fancy leads them. Imagine how happily they are absorbed in finding just the right outfit to make her look as radiant a bride as she can be.

CHAPTER FIFTEEN

Stepmembers of the Wedding

What do you do if a future stepdaughter is too old to be a flower girl and too young for a bridesmaid but she wants to take part in your wedding? This is a time for you to sort out your priorities. If that perfect wedding would be marred for you by a twelve-year-old flower girl, or a preteen bridesmaid, you just may have to explain this to your fiancé's daughter. Or you could make an exception in her case. Only you can weigh how important is the perfection of the composition of the wedding party and the significance of this situation in your relationship with your future husband's daughter. Whatever you decide, think it through carefully and talk it over thoroughly with your fiancé before talking to his daughter.

Another problem that often arises is the request of a child to invite the other parent to the wedding. Margie, an advertising executive with no children of her own, was marrying a man with a teenaged son from a previous marriage.

"My fiancé kept assuring his son that our marriage would make no difference in their relationship, nor the friendship he and his ex-wife had." As though to test those promises, "Jeff asked his dad if he could invite his mother to our wedding," Margie explained.

At first Margie seriously considered going along with the boy. But in talking it over with her friends, Margie realized how much she *didn't* want her fiancé's ex-wife at the wedding. Upset, she consulted a child psychologist whose advice was that Margie not have at her wedding a woman whose presence would make her feel uncomfortable. The therapist also suggested that Margie make her feelings definitely known to her fiancé. Then together they should kindly, but firmly, tell his son that his mother couldn't come to the wedding, explaining the reasons simply and clearly.

Whenever children are involved in a wedding, the engaged couple has to make choices between their own preferences and the needs of the children. This balancing act can be either divisive or unifying for the couple, depending on how they handle it. Even if there is only one set of children, conflicts are bound to erupt, but when each of you is a parent, the potential for divided loyalties and unpleasant misunderstandings quickly multiplies. Keep in mind that, like so many other aspects of the wedding, how these issues are resolved can predict the way in which they will be dealt with in the marriage. The pattern you set now can determine how you manage the merging of two separate families later on.

The only way you can keep the lines of communication open is for you and your fiancé to talk over the children's role in the wedding. It's important that you understand each other's thoughts and feelings on the subject so that the kids don't find an opportunity to drive a wedge between you. Once you're in the habit of talking it all out, you will be acting in accordance with decisions mutually agreed upon, and the possibilities of misunderstandings will be minimized.

The first thing you need to agree on is to keep your expectations realistic. Your children are probably *not* going to accept this wedding with an unqualified delight, no matter how well you handle the situation. Children's conflicting loyalties between the marrying parent and the other parent go with the territory of remarriage, even if the first marriage ended in death rather than divorce. Once this reality is faced, you'll both stop demanding the impossible of yourselves—and of them.

The next point of agreement should be to include the children in the wedding plans from the very beginning. You have already told them of your engagement before announcing the news to anyone else. Now it is necessary to keep them informed of all your plans. But you can do a lot more than simply impart information. Having your children involved in the decision-making processes will make them feel like participants rather than bystanders at your nuptials.

Even very young children can be given some choices. You can ask them their preferences about serving roast beef or turkey for the main course at the wedding dinner. Or which ice cream is to be served with the wedding cake—chocolate and vanilla, or vanilla and strawberry? Don't make your question open-ended by asking something like, what should we serve at the dinner? Such an overall query is putting too much responsibility on the child. Whatever the nature of the question, it should be a valid one, and not simply an abstract exercise, no matter what the age of the child is. There should be a real question and it should be phrased in a sufficiently limited style that you will be able to accept whatever answer is given and implement it. Therefore, unless you want to run the risk of serving pistachio ice cream at your reception, limit the choice of ice creams to those which would be acceptable to you.

You and the groom may want to make a list of questions you wish to ask each child, keeping in mind careful and proscribed phrasing as well as the age and interests of the particular child. If either of you has a child with a well-developed aesthetic sense, you may want to ask him or her to choose the colors of the flowers from among those which are acceptable to you. If you want your invitations printed only on cream-colored or pure white stationery but either of these would suit you, this could be another appropriate selection for a child to make.

If any of your children like research tasks, you might ask them to check with their geography teacher about a few Caribbean islands, provided you have already narrowed down your choices for a honeymoon location. If one of you has a teenaged girl with a flair for fashion, you could take her along when you buy your wedding dress. A young boy with an interest in music could gather information which would help you select a band for your reception. If you are having an informal gathering with the music coming from your stereo system, you might ask a musical offspring to serve as the disc jockey. An artistic son or daughter can help with the wedding decorations, or even design the invitations.

"My eight-year-old daughter did a wonderfully vibrant painting of a wedding, and we had it printed on the outside cover of the cards we used for invitations," said a bride who was determined to include her children in her wedding preparations to the fullest extent possible.

Whenever possible, take the children with you on visits to caterers, travel agents, and possible wedding sites. This doesn't mean *all* the children *all* the time. If there are two sets of kids, it may be advisable to take them on separate trips, but don't force any child to go along if he or she doesn't want to. Try to make these outings special, perhaps beginning with a meal at a restaurant the children like, and concluding with a movie they want to see. Whenever possible, involve children with aspects of the wedding plans in which they are most interested.

Whether or not the children are interested in clothing, however, their apparel for the wedding should be discussed with them, and for all but the youngest children, should be purchased with them. Children shouldn't be made to feel that you have selected the clothing you want them to wear without ascertaining their preferences, and you should adhere to these preferences whenever possible. Another area where you can make children feel a valued part of the wedding is to let each of them invite a best friend to be their special guest. The selection of this guest should be discussed, and the child given the invitation to address and send out him or herself.

A cautionary note should be sounded here. Not every child will *want* to be involved in the wedding preparations. Your excellent intentions and skilled use of child psychology notwithstanding, ambivalent feelings about this wedding will exist in all the children. Should any of them express the wish to be left alone about the whole event, you should honor this request. Make clear that later participation is always welcomed, but that no one is going to be pushed into being a part of the planning if he or she doesn't want to be. Your wedding is a joyful occasion, and help with it should only be given willingly.

The other error to avoid with children is one that anxious parents often make before their second wedding. Eager to please reluctant children, they end up placating. Don't leave so much up to the children and appear so dependent on their cooperation that you let them feel too strong a sense of power over the unfolding events. This feeling of having too much control is anxiety-producing in children and will only exacerbate their ambivalence. This is, after all, *your* wedding, and it will take place with or without their approval. You want to reassure them that they are not being excluded. Encourage their participation, but don't go overboard and plead for their acceptance as this will only prove counterproductive.

How much the children will participate in the wedding ceremony itself should be thoroughly talked over between you and your fiancé before discussing it with them. The more informal your wedding, the more chance there will be for their participation. A mother of two children who was marrying a father of three, Rosemary had all five children stand up with her and the groom when they exchanged their vows. She described her first wedding as "big on form, low on feelings," and her second as "chockful of all the good emotions."

If you have opted for the kind of informality which permits you to have all the offspring gathered around you, some thorny problems will be avoided. If, on the other hand, you have your heart set on a formal wedding, there is a greater chance that the children will feel excluded.

Alison, an assistant district attorney in her early thirties who was divorced and had no children, married a man who had two daughters, eleven and thirteen. "My first wedding was so understated that it didn't even feel like I was getting married," she said ruefully. "The second time, I wanted a real wedding, with my four closest friends as bridesmaids and my sister as matron of honor. But my fiancé's daughters wanted to be bridesmaids. Even if they had been older, I would still have had a problem because I'd already chosen my bridesmaids," Alison said in a tone of exasperation.

Susan, another second-time bride, faced similar issues, but her situation was different from Alison's because Susan had children from her first marriage. It was Susan's sincere wish that her best friend and her teenage daughter be her bridesmaids. Her fiancé wanted his college-age son to be his best man. However, what roles would the younger children play?

If you find yourself facing similar problems as you plan your wedding, it is essential for you and your fiancé to first talk the issues over openly and honestly between yourselves, and then with all the children involved. You can find other duties for children not included in the wedding ceremony itself, such as ushering in the guests. Children need not be included in the wedding march for them to have as full a sense of participation in the ceremony as they have had in its planning stages.

One creative mother's second wedding took place in the summer, under a big tree at the country club where the reception was held. She wore a white cotton gown of striking simplicity and carried red roses. Her four children, who escorted guests to their seats but did not stand up before the minister, all wore variations on that color scheme. Her daughters wore white gowns and also held red roses; her sons wore white suits and sported red carnations.

It is, of course, for you and your groom to decide who is in your wedding party. And it is also for you to decide if the price in unhappiness and hurt feelings is too high for certain choices to be ultimately desirable. These are the tough decisions that make second weddings so dynamic a challenge, testing your sensitivity and ingenuity in confronting subtle complications and stubborn obstacles.

If you feel you have to say no to a child's request to directly participate in the ceremony, deal with the hurt feelings as they are expressed and don't inhibit their expression. Keep the lines of communication open and encourage suggestions from all sources. But don't be apologetic or obsequious with your disappointed child or future stepchild. Don't give way to feelings of guilt. Once you and your fiancé have made a decision, don't agonize about it by yourself, or rehash it between yourselves. As long as the relationship between parent and child is basically sound, disappointments won't be overwhelming.

If there are fundamental problems in the relationship, marching down an aisle won't make them go away. When children insist on a particular role in the wedding party, try to find out what they are really saying. In some cases, a child may be testing to see how much control he or she can exert over this wedding. In other instances, the child can be expressing anxieties about being excluded from the parent's new life. When you understand the origin of the insistence, you are better able to handle it.

Remember that including the children in the wedding doesn't begin with their role in the ceremony itself. It starts when you and your fiancé announce your engagement. It deepens as you include them in the planning process, soliciting their opinions, requesting their help in specific areas, and drawing them into the decision-making processes. If the betrothed couple is committed to finding a meaningful participation for each child involved, fears of being excluded will be kept to a minimum.

The prenuptial period can be one in which family members are drawn together rather than pulled apart, provided sufficient effort is consistently made in that direction. At the wedding itself, it is up to the bride and groom and to every other adult present to be sensitive to the needs of children and include them in the merriment and joy. If you and your new husband sincerely feel the children are an inherent part of this second marriage, you can convey that conviction to them. Then they will truly feel themselves a part of this new family you are creating.

CHAPTER SIXTEEN

Standing on Ceremony

The role given both sets of children in the ceremony will be determined by the size and style of your wedding. A maid or matron of honor followed by a retinue of bridesmaids is often more appropriate for a first wedding than a second. In a second wedding, either another couple who are close to both bride and groom will walk down the aisle before them, or if there is no such couple, you may have a sister or a very good friend walk with the best man. Sometimes the groom chooses his son to be the best man. You may want your daughter or your about-to-be stepdaughter to follow the maid of honor and the best man, and precede you down the aisle.

When you are tailoring tradition to make everybody happy, the most informal wedding can have a flower girl. What little girl doesn't like to be the center of attention as she strews rose petals in the bride's path? You can also have two flower girls if there are two such children in your family. One woman had her groom's teenage daughter serve as maid of honor. The young girl walked down the stairs of the bride's best friend's house, in which the ceremony was being held, and was then followed by the small daughter of the bride and the small son of the hostess. The delighted children walked hand in hand, preceding the bride, who walked down the stairs by herself to join her groom and the minister at the hearth, which was serving as the altar.

Whether you walk alone, or on the arm of your father or another man, is another question for you to decide. The father of the bride giving his daughter away is an ancient custom almost universally observed in first weddings. The second wedding is quite another matter. First of all, the bride is older and her father may not be living. If this is the case with you but you like the idea of being accompanied by a male relative, there is surely an uncle or brother or brother-in-law who would be honored to give you his arm on that special walk down the aisle.

Other second-time brides prefer to go it alone, even if they have a living father. Such was the case with Joyce, a high school principal in her forties and the mother of two children in college. "I'd been supporting myself and my children for so many years since my first husband walked out on us that it seemed absurd for my father to be giving me away," she explained. Joyce talked it over with her father first and ascertained that he understood her feelings and wasn't hurt. "Dad said he is so proud of the way I took charge of my life after I was divorced and brought my kids up by myself that he *wanted* to see me walk down the aisle as proud and independent as I've been all this time."

Another woman, Leann, let her father walk her down the aisle because they were estranged at her first wedding, which he didn't attend. "I knew how badly my father had felt about those quarrels back then and how important to him was the chance to have me on his arm at my wedding," Leann said with a smile at the memory of the happiness her gesture gave her father.

Asking a man other than your father to walk down the aisle with you can be a loving gesture to someone you care about. Kate did just that when she asked the older brother who had lent her the money to go to law school to accompany her down the aisle instead of her stepfather, with whom she had never been close. Roslyn felt that way about the boss who had been her mentor at work.

"He was a father figure to me in the career which had been my whole life between my marriages," said Roslyn, who was married for a few years in her early twenties and then single till her second marriage in her late thirties. Since her first marriage produced no children, and her social life always took a backseat to her work, Roslyn was making two kinds of statements when she asked her boss to give her away. On the more obvious level, she was paying a kind of homage to the man who had believed in her and encouraged her in a challenging endeavor. But there was a subtler meaning to her choice. "My work had been everything to me, but now I was entering a new phase in my life in which my commitment to the man I was marrying would be even more significant than my dedication to my career," Roslyn said thoughtfully. "Somehow having my boss hand me over to my groom symbolized for me that shift in my priorities."

All rituals are, by definition, rife with symbolism and the wedding ceremony is no exception. For this reason, choosing who will participate in yours is far more than a perfunctory social decision. When a woman marries for the first time, she and her friends all take very seriously who will be asked to be bridesmaids, and especially the maid of honor, unless she has a sister to fill that position. Your closest friend, who has seen you through all the tough times, will not be hurt if you ask the sixteen-year-old girl who is soon to be your stepdaughter to precede you down the aisle. She will understand that this girl is going through a tough time of her own, and that giving her a key role in the ceremony is your way of offering her your friendship.

Since every aspect of this second wedding is a subject for discussion between you and your groom, the two of you should talk about questions of who stands up for him. Will the best man be your teenage son, who badly needs to feel he has a central part in this event, or will it be the groom's closest friend? Resist the temptation to push a choice on your fiancé which is not truly his. Just as you wouldn't want him to pressure you to have his daughter be your maid of honor, he doesn't need you to wage a campaign in favor of your son's candidacy for best man. A neat, smooth solution can't be found for every dilemma, and you'll have to allow for some rough edges.

The point to keep in mind is that in any wedding, it is the bride's decision who her attendant(s) are and the groom's prerogative to select his. Your priorities in making these choices may have changed as you have matured, but these choices remain yours to make for yourself—and your groom's for himself. If *you* would far rather have your sister than your groom's daughter march down the aisle, follow the dictates of your own preference. And give the man you are marrying the same autonomy. Feeling caught in a morass of conflicting emotional tugs, don't lose sight of the fact that this is your wedding.

Of course, the more informal your wedding ceremony, the fewer of these tricky choices will you have to make. "We didn't want a lot of ushers and bridesmaids," said Angela, the second-time bride of a third-time groom. "But narrowing it down to one best man and one maid or matron of honor was causing us too many conflicts, so we simplified the whole thing." At Angela's wedding, the bride and groom suddenly appeared hand-in-hand amid the assembled guests and everyone formed a circle around them and the officiating clergyman. "That way we didn't have to make choices between our siblings, stepchildren, and dearest friends," Angela happily explained. "We were encircled by the warmth and best wishes of everyone we care about."

Another alternative to a formal processional or none at all is to let everyone who feels like walking down the aisle do so. Linda found this worked very well for her. "At first Josh and I were just going to have the couple who introduced us walk down the aisle," she recalled. The "aisle" in this case was the corridor of her cousin's country house leading from the front parlor to the living room where the guests were assembled. Linda, a Protestant, was marrying Joshua, who was Jewish, in a ceremony conducted by the justice of the peace for the township in which her cousin lived. While both families accepted the civil ceremony, Linda knew it was causing her fiancé's parents some pain.

"Josh was their oldest son and for him this was a first wedding," Linda said. When Josh explained to her that in a traditional Jewish wedding the groom's parents walk down the aisle with him between them, Linda invited her future in-laws to escort their son to his place beside her.

Another bride, more concerned with people's feelings than questions of protocol, invited her mother and her grandmother to walk down the aisle of the church together. The grandmother had only recently recovered from a serious illness and was so thrilled at being able to attend her granddaughter's second wedding that the bride wanted to give her a special role in the ceremony. The bride's six-year-old daughter from her first marriage served as flower girl, which meant that four generations of women from their family stood at the altar together.

If you're going to have several people marching in your wedding procession, a rehearsal is usually a good idea, followed by a buffet supper. Such a gathering need not be restricted simply to those who are going to be participating in the ceremony as it would be in a more formal and elaborate first wedding. An easygoing dinner is the perfect time to get together with some of the people who might be more comfortable meeting before the wedding, such as your past and future in-laws, or your sister's teenage daughter who would get a chance to meet your fiancé's daughter of the same age. Or the two sets of stepkids could invite some friends of their own.

Of course, you can throw this friendly post-rehearsal party yourself. But if your mother is itching to do a bit of hostessing, maybe she could invite everyone over to her house for a hearty meal featuring her famous meatloaf. Or for a complete break with convention, the groom might like to do the honors by whipping up some supper for this disparate group of friends and relatives. Perhaps there's a good friend of yours who lives near the rehearsal site and wants to ask you all over for a Chinese take-out dinner.

The more informal you keep this rehearsal party, the easier it will be to dissolve tensions as former and future relatives— often a complex assortment of exes—mix and mingle in this wedding preview. If there are going to be any potentially awkward introductions, they will be made much smoother in a simple, down-to-earth atmosphere. This kind of gathering will do much to set the tone of warmth and solidity for the impending wedding, and will prove a meaningful rehearsal on several levels of social interaction.

Your wedding can be highly individualized if you find a way to personalize the ceremony itself. One way is for you and your groom to select the music you want played as the guests arrive and when the bridal party is coming down the aisle. You can hire any number and type of musicians, from a solo saxophonist specializing in your favorite jazz piece to a violin trio. A rock band is a possibility, as is an organist with a passion for Bach. The only criterion is that the music be personally meaningful to the bridal pair.

Another way to personalize the ceremony is for the bride and groom to exchange vows they wrote themselves. This practice is becoming increasingly frequent for first weddings, and is even more fitting for second weddings when the couple is mature enough to be aware of what's special about their relationship, and able to express their feelings. Personalizing the exchange of vows gives the two of you a chance to share with those who care most about you what it is you value most in each other.

If yours is to be a civil ceremony, you can add a spiritual dimension if you wish by inserting biblical quotations into your vows. If your wedding is being performed by a clergyman, it is still permissible to personalize the ritual. Ministers, priests, and rabbis have no objection to couples adding phrases of their own to the service, but they do have some problems with deletions, as there are specific words which each religion dictates be included in the marriage ceremony. Couples planning to write their own vows in a religious ceremony are advised to consult with the clergyman who will be conducting the service and make certain that there is no conflict. If there are nuances in the vows you have written which are problematic for an older, more conservative pastor, you have the option of choosing another more liberal associate.

When the ceremony is a civil one and you have no interest in bringing religious sentiments into it, you can infuse the prosaic legal phrases with the warmth and depth of your romantic feelings. The vows you write can also contain a simple statement of the values by which you and your beloved wish to conduct your married life. You can even look at the writing of your vows as an exercise in expressing the beliefs and feelings which are most important to you. Writing them together can be a sweetly meaningful experience. Another possibility is to write them separately, and then you can surprise each other with the words you have chosen to say.

It's important to remember that a wedding ceremony is a public event, sanctioned by the state, often in conjunction with an established religion. Unless you have gone off to some European hideaway or tropical paradise, you are sharing this ceremony with significant people in both your lives. Therefore, however romantic the sentiments expressed in your personal statement, it is not a private exchange of emotions, but a public declaration of your commitment. In other words, the phrases you write shouldn't sound like the words of a popular love song, but rather should be a coherently conceived, sincerely presented statement of your feelings about each other and your ideals about married life.

If this idea appeals to you but you have some trepidation

about your ability to succinctly write your thoughts on subjects of such depth and delicacy, don't despair. Start by jotting down your thoughts and feelings, then take time to expand, polish, and refine your notes. Quotations can help. The wise man Kahlil Gibran, in his poetic and profound collection of teachings called *The Prophet*, offers some moving and thought-provoking passages on marriage. Or you may turn to the Romantic poets for inspiration—consider, for example, Robert Browning's immortal line: "Grow old along with me! The best is yet to be." A literary friend, or perhaps your local librarian, could be of help in finding suitable quotations.

A few brief, well-chosen phrases can convey a universe of thought and feelings. While you may not care to strip your soul in public, you might want to share with those who are participating in your joy something of the private history which has led to this precious moment. One second-time bride, who had been alone for a number of years following the dissolution of her first marriage, faced the man to whom she was totally committing herself and said:

> *Because you have brought so much joy into my life and taught me the healing power of love, have shown me how to trust and feel and give the best that is in me freely and fearlessly, I pledge to you my unswerving devotion and the love which will be yours for as long as I live.*

Another bride was touched to tears when her groom, who had lost his first wife in the prime of their lives to a terrible illness, spoke of how this new love had given him back his faith in God and capacity for happiness. And a woman widowed by an automobile accident shared with the assembled wedding guests how her new husband's tenderness had rescued her from the prison of grief and trauma in which she had been trapped. Such poignant statements are terribly moving and can be a cathartic moment in uniting a new family, but a public expression of intense personal feeling is not for everyone. Only express what is comfortable for you to share with others, but don't hold back feelings you want to share because of inhibitions.

For those who don't want to touch on the past, a statement of how you will live your married life can be effective and enlightening. For example, one bride told her groom:

> *I promise to be there for you in whatever way you need me so that your dreams become my purpose. In joy and sorrow, tears and laughter, I will strive to be as one with you so that there be no veil between our souls. Savoring the good times together, sharing the bad, I will rejoice in the glow of your health and sustain you through the pale of sickness. My will serves your wishes, my mind seeks yours and my heart I give you this day with all the love it can hold.*

After you and your groom exchange your vows, it is possible to ask others around you to comment on what your union means to them. There is a tradition for this in the Quaker meeting, an informal meditation session in which anyone present can express his or her thoughts aloud. Such a request for spontaneous remarks from the members of your wedding party and the assembled guests can prove an enriching experience for all involved. Many second weddings often follow a period of loss because the first marriage ended in either a disillusioning divorce, or a tragic death. A new love forged from the ashes of the old can be an inspiration to those who see its strength and beauty. Encouraging others to express what your love means to them creates a sense of community and continuity.

Should this idea appeal to you, it might be a good idea to let one or two particularly articulate relatives and friends in on the plan so that the request for comments doesn't meet with an awkward silence. This request can come either from one or the other of the bridal couple, or from the civil or religious official performing the ceremony. If older children are grouped around you, they might want to know beforehand that there will be an opportunity to express their feelings, but be sure no one is made to feel such an expression is expected. You're not seeking testimonials, but heartfelt remarks.

When deciding whether or not to involve the assembled guests in your ceremony, consider your family and friends. Make sure that such a ritual is one with which they would feel comfortable. Do what feels right for you and for those you love.

CHAPTER SEVENTEEN

Reception Essentials

Flowers, food, music, and photos are the essential ingredients of any wedding reception, and you'll want your choices in these to enhance the individualized quality of your second nuptials.

Flowers

Flowers are the stuff of wedding magic, and in second weddings their selection can be much more varied than in first-time nuptials.

"Stay away from the pale pinks and the whites," suggests Tom Sakas, owner of Manhattan's Gramercy Park Flower Shop, which does the floral arrangements for many of New York's most stylish second weddings. Sakas believes in going for a more sophisticated and original flower decor, which would certainly fit in well with the whole tone of your second nuptials. He favors brighter colors than the traditional bridal pastel flower shades, believing that deeper pinks, yellows, and reds are more appropriate to a second wedding.

Since you're not as likely to be marrying in the late spring or early summer as a first-time bride, you can take advantage of the less frequently displayed flowers of other seasons. For an autumn wedding Sakas suggests "a very rustic grapevine basket with big vines, autumn leaves, moss rock. The flowers, whose stems should pierce through the basket, are cymbidium orchids, which are small and yellow and grow about twenty flowers to a branch, and Rothschild lilies, magenta, yellow-striped flowers."

For a winter wedding, Sakas offers a unique centerpiece with a highly contemporary look in a fashionable Oriental style. In a black ceramic dish, he places black Japanese river stones, a piece of curly willow, three to five lavender orchids, and a big green leaf draping over the sides.

A great fan of the "English country garden look," Sakas says its style will work well for any wedding, whatever the season. In autumn, this look, which is very much in vogue, can be achieved by mixing mums, lilies, and roses. For a spring or summer wedding, this same look could easily be put together by baskets fully but loosely packed with flowers which spill over the sides of the baskets, making them invisible. These baskets, containing wild flowers of the season like lilacs, Queen Anne's lace, and wild roses, are moderately priced. For a more exotic touch, Peruvian lilies and African daisies can be added to these fragrant baskets.

If you're having a country wedding in the warm weather months, family and friends can purchase baskets and pick wild flowers to fill them. These baskets are a wonderful gift for the budget-conscious bride and groom, and make a lovely decoration for all the tables at the wedding reception. For the price-minded urban bride, a tour of the wholesale flower market district of your city with a green-thumbed friend should produce some terrific purchases at great discount.

Because second weddings often don't take place in a church, florists don't get many requests for flowers to fill the pews from second-time brides. Instead, the emphasis is on the floral arrangements for the tables at the reception. Sakas uses a pair of nine-foot laurel branches to create "a fantasy rose-bush," of Doris Riker roses, a tall cluster of cabbage-shaped roses in a peachy pink, with cattleya orchids, white petals with lavender centers, dispersed among them.

Contemporary floral concepts can be of immense help if you want to carry flowers at the wedding ceremony but don't want the traditional bridal bouquet you had at your first wedding. Sakas suggests that such a bride carry a cluster of roses, their stems showing and tied with a green velvet ribbon. An off-white shade such as that of champagne roses is very appealing. If you want a more vivid color, you can carry a special kind of French rose called the Nicole, which is dark red on the outside and white on the inside. Should you want to be more exotic, a cluster of Hawaiian dendrobium orchids are breath-takingly lovely. Twenty to thirty lavender-and-white flowers grow on each stem and the stems range from twelve to eighteen inches. If, on the other hand, your floral tastes run in simpler directions, a cluster of lilacs and peonies is perfect for the second-time bride to carry in her arms at a spring wedding.

Like every other aspect of this second wedding, flower traditions should give way to a more personal approach. "When I got married the first time, my husband gave me my bridal bouquet, composed, naturally, of all white flowers, because it is the groom's traditional gift to his bride," said Rachel, a psychologist embarking on her second marriage at thirty-seven. "This time, at the ceremony, I'll be carrying a cluster of wild flowers picked and arranged by my cousin who's a botanist. Since the man I'm marrying has been with me every step of the way in planning this wedding, we don't feel any need for him to be the one who gives me the flowers. It makes more sense for that gift to come from the person in my life who knows flowers best and will be picking them in the woods just for me."

However, there are other traditions which may hold a charm for you and fit in easily with the informal style of your second wedding. Customarily, the groom's boutonniere complements the bride's bouquet. If you're not carrying a bouquet but have, for instance, pinned a corsage of white roses on the 1940s classic navy suit you're wearing for your winter wedding, you can put one of those roses in your groom's buttonhole. Such a gesture is perfectly in keeping with the motto of your second wedding: If the tradition fits your needs, wear it; if not, alter it until it suits you.

Food

In a thematic wedding, the food choices come naturally to mind. If your wedding has a nautical theme and is being held at a yacht club, a luncheon of lobster salad preceded by platters of shrimp cocktail and clams on the half shell would be perfectly appropriate. For a wedding brunch with a distinctly Western flavor, eggs ranchero or refried beans and tacos would be original and apt. If your wedding is a mixture of styles rather than one which follows the thread of a single theme, the setting can often solve the problem of what to serve. A private club will frequently offer you a choice of several possible nuptial meals, as will a hotel, or a caterer hired for a home wedding.

You can also let your food preferences determine the place you pick to hold the reception. If you and your fiancé are fond of the cuisine of a particular nationality, you can hold the reception at a restaurant featuring that type of food.

"Although neither Ken nor I are Greek," a lively art director named Phyllis said, "we both adore Greek food, so we found an authentic taverna and held our reception there. The waiters served a marvelous moussaka and then spontaneously did their traditional dances for us." Since many of Ken and Phyllis's guests had imbibed sufficient quantities of ouzo to dissolve their inhibitions, they joined in the dancing, "which just goes to prove," Phyllis concluded with a shrug and a grin, "that you don't have to be Greek to have a Greek wedding!"

Another couple, with a strong penchant for Japanese food, arranged to hold their reception at the best Japanese restaurant in their city. From sushi bar to steaks prepared in front of the assembled guests in traditional style, the repast was completely Japanese. While planning the wedding with the restaurant's owner, the bride became intrigued with other aspects of Japanese culture and at the last minute decided to wear a ceremonial kimono rather than the two-piece crepe de chine dress she'd bought.

Sometimes you can select a setting for sentimental reasons rather than culinary ones but still end up with an exotic feast which is immensely popular with your guests. Such was the case with Stan and Beverly, who had many happy dinner dates in an Indian restaurant located close to both their offices.

"It was there, lingering over irresistibly sweet desserts and strong Indian tea, that we really opened up to each other and talked honestly about our feelings, which had been badly hurt in our first marriages, and our fears of becoming romantically involved again. Later, it was in that same restaurant that Stan asked me to marry him," Beverly related with a flush of happiness at the memory.

Much as Stan and Beverly wanted to have their wedding reception at the Indian restaurant, they were reluctant to offer such foreign fare to their meat-and-potatoes families. A consultation with the restaurant's owner produced a compromise. "The chef made several dishes in which he cut back on the stronger spices and also offered an alternative menu of American food," Beverly explained.

That way the gourmet palates of the couple's urbane friends were sufficiently stimulated, while the more prosaic taste buds of their parents weren't too challenged. Not only was the food a tremendous success all around, but having their reception in the setting where they first fell in love was romantic and meaningful.

Food, lovingly prepared, can be a significant contribution to a wedding. This is reason enough to consider an at-home reception in which family and friends are invited to bring their culinary specialties for a bountiful buffet. This kind of repast can go a long way toward smoothing ruffled familial feathers while contributing to the ambience of warmth and individuality which you want for your second wedding.

"My new mother-in-law, a traditional Italian-American housewife, was horrified that we weren't having a church ceremony," recalls Kimberly Warren of her wedding to Joe Santini. "A daughter-in-law who was the divorced mother of three children and vice-president of a personnel agency was hardly her idea of a fitting bride for her son. But the way my friends took to her lasagna went a long way toward making Joe's mother feel less of a stranger to our lifestyle."

Even if you have a formal, catered reception, there's no reason why some goodies can't be contributed by caring friends and relatives. One couple, who had a small stylish ceremony at an exclusive private club followed by a fashionable reception there, arranged with the staff to let the groom's mother prepare some of her immensely popular chopped chicken liver. Another bridal pair had their wedding party at a trendy restaurant which permitted the bride's closest friend to bring her homemade chocolate mousse, which turned out to be better than the wedding cake itself.

If you're planning a catered dinner, be aware of your guests' food requirements. Because the backgrounds of your friends and families are probably more diversified at this second wedding than was the case in your homogeneous first nuptials, take into consideration which foods are forbidden to whom. A vegetarian alternative to a roast beef dinner would be a thoughtful gesture if you are inviting guests who don't eat meat, as would a kosher meal for religious Jewish relatives. If your reception is a catered cocktail party, make certain the hors d'oeuvres will appeal to a wide variety of tastes.

Music

The music played at your wedding will do much to establish the atmosphere you wish. Few things are as expressive of a couple's personal style as the kind of music they enjoy. If your musical tastes are different, you can have two kinds of music. Perhaps a ragtime piano for the cocktail hour followed by a string quartet specializing in chamber music for the sit-down dinner.

The music for thematic weddings should fit in with the theme. One couple who had a Roaring Twenties theme hired a band which played the "Charleston," to which the bridesmaids, dressed as flappers, performed a well-rehearsed dance routine. Ethnic themes call for ethnic music, which doesn't mean you have to be corny. If you are having an Irish wedding, hire a few fiddlers and other musicians to play authentic Irish folk songs, which are a far cry from popular tunes like "Galway Bay" and "When Irish Eyes Are Smiling." If you want a string quartet which plays only Mozart, the musicians could wear eighteenth-century costumes you provide. If you were a teenager in the fifties and nostalgia for your youth prompts you to hire a band specializing in fifties music, try to get them to dress accordingly so they look like the cast for *Grease* as they belt out Chuck Berry and Elvis hits. You can do the same for the sounds of the sixties, and have the band decked out in tie-dyed splendor under psychedelic lighting.

Of course, if you're having dancing at the reception, you'll want a band which can play a variety of dance music, and you may want to take your guests' musical tastes into consideration. But don't lose sight of whose wedding this is. Play the music which is most meaningful to you. Perhaps a particular kind of music has been an important common interest for you both, then surely you will want to hear it on your wedding day. If the music you chose for your bridal procession is also suitable for the reception, have it continued. If devotion to Dixieland bands has always been a bond between you, by all means have one at your wedding. Maybe it won't mean much to your kids, for whom music begins and ends with Heavy Metal, or your parents with their penchant for popular show tunes, but this isn't their wedding. If you want to dance to Strauss waltzes early in the evening and frug to more contemporary sounds as the night wears on, do so. If your musical tastes are eclectic, have a band which can play a wide variety of songs.

Or don't have a band at all. With good hi-fi equipment, and maybe a young wedding guest who's an aspiring DJ, you can play your favorite groups to your heart's content. One couple, still hooked on the music of their youth, came down the aisle to the sounds of the Beatles' "Lucy in the Sky with Diamonds," and then took their vows while John Lennon sang "Imagine" in the background. At the informal reception following the ceremony, the guest doubling as DJ played choice albums of the sixties to which the guests danced for hours. If you've received a CD player for a wedding present, along with your favorite albums made so much more vivid on CD, now might be a good time to show off your new equipment and collection. You might want to consider the possibility of calling the local radio station which plays your favorite music and see if you can hire the DJ services of an expert in the sounds of your choice.

As with food and flowers, music can be a precious gift for loved ones to bestow on the bridal pair. A friend's rendition of your favorite folk songs on a guitar or a group of friends forming a choral group and singing some German lieder they've rehearsed for your wedding pleasure are examples of gifts of talent, which can mean so much. This does *not* mean that your cousin's daughter who's had a semester of accordion lessons or a nephew whose accomplishments on the violin barely border on the mediocre should be asked for their musical contributions. This isn't amateur hour, nor is it that first wedding where familial wishes override the expression of the bride and groom's taste and judgment. Only those family and friends whose instrument playing and singing voices have a sweet and

147

special meaning for the two of you, as well as possessing an intrinsic musical value, should be invited to play and sing at your wedding.

Photos

Of course, you will want a photographer, either a hired professional or an amateur friend making you a present of his or her talents to take photos of your nuptials. But there's more that can be done with picture taking than simply having a camera record the highlights of the ceremony and reception.

"Because I'd been married before, the idea of an album beginning with the bride putting on her veil in front of her mirror the morning of the wedding, and ending with everyone waving goodbye to the newlyweds as they drive away, didn't exactly thrill me," said Meredith, an associate editor at a fashion magazine.

Since the groom's teenage son was a photography buff with a collection of costly cameras and his own darkroom, the couple made good use of his hobby.

"Ricky took pictures of all our preparations—of Richard and I getting the marriage license at City Hall, talking to the minister in his study, visiting banquet halls, travel agents, and jewelry stores," Meredith recalled. There was even a picture of each of them getting a blood test. Her future stepson took photos of Meredith modeling various wedding outfits, and buying a dress for a niece who was going to be the flower girl. Photos were taken of the bridal shower Meredith's friends threw for her, of the engagement party the groom's brother gave the couple, of the wedding rehearsal, and the supper party following it. The wedding day marked the middle of the album rather than the end of it, and it recorded a series of events that took place over several weeks rather than a few hours.

Another innovative use of photographs at a wedding was

the way one enterprising bride made a collage of photographs taken of her and the groom over the several years they had known each other. These were blown up and then hung on the wall of the restaurant where the reception was held. And there's still another photographic idea you may want to try which can serve as surprise gift to your groom. Obtain baby, childhood, adolescent, and young adult pictures of each of you, and hang them on the walls of the room where your reception is being held. This display can make a touching statement about how your past separate lives have grown into your present unity. It will also prove to be an excellent conversation piece at the reception, particularly when the bride's and/or groom's parents don't know many of the other guests. Questions about the pictures can be a great conversational ice breaker.

High-tech equipment such as VCRs are, of course, becoming a standard feature at weddings. Perhaps you have a friend or relative who fancies him or herself a movie director, and who is creative with a video camera. Let that person tape your wedding, from close-ups of the ceremony, to long-distance shots of the bridal couple driving off into the sunset. If the tape turns out well, you could have a few copies made to be given to special relatives and closest friends. Or maybe the man or woman with a camera would present you and those closest to you with tapes of the occasion.

One couple tried an interesting video experiment which worked. "Actually, it was Nick's daughter's idea," said Rita, a conservative corporate executive in her mid-forties, and newly married to the father of Cristy, a film school student in her early twenties. "For a special video project Cristy wanted to tape conversations with us and the rest of the family for a few days prior to the wedding," Nick explained.

"At first, I found it unnerving, an invasion of privacy," Rita said frankly, "but after a short time, I forgot the camera was there and now I must say that I'm very pleased and impressed with the result of Cristy's work."

149

The result was two hours of video tape in which the viewer saw everything from a flurry of last-minute wedding preparations to impromptu interviews with various members of the family. Some of these, like the talks with Rita's teenage children, whose father died of cancer several years earlier, have a raw and painful quality, but they also serve to intensify the glow of happiness on Rita's face as she hugs Nick the night before their wedding. Cristy captured candid moments of joy and anticipation, as well as the shadows of sad memories flickering across smiling faces. It's best, however, to avoid slick video pros who will want you to adjust the style and schedule of your ceremony to fit their production requirements.

If the idea of taping segments of family conversations and preparations in those frenetic days preceding the wedding is appealing, you will have a treasured keepsake in the years to come. You might include you and your groom sitting on the living room couch the evening before the wedding, talking about how you feel about each other and your impending marriage. Think how much such a tape would mean to you ten, twenty, or thirty years later. If you are planning children, a taped record of you before your wedding, and then on your wedding day, would be thrilling for your children to see as they grow up.

Photos and videos enhance and sharpen memories. They provide a vivid record of your happiest day which will always be there for you. If there is no one to take pictures and make tapes of your wedding among your friends and relatives, hire someone to do it. Cut costs somewhere else if you have to, but don't deny yourselves the future pleasure of reliving this day through photographs and video tapes. You'll find the expense was well worth it every time you take out your wedding album, or slip the cassette of your nuptials into your VCR, for a heartwarming trip down memory lane.

CHAPTER EIGHTEEN

Reception Etiquette

Many traditions associated with a wedding take place at the reception. Think of them as choices from which you can select, keeping what strikes your fancy, discarding what looks like it won't work for what you have in mind.

The bridal party receiving line is just one example of where custom might bend a bit. Even if you are having a formal wedding, you might want to dispense with a formal receiving line and, after the ceremony, go up to those around you, embracing everyone in turn and exchanging the kind of heartfelt comments which the rigid protocol of a receiving line might inhibit. Instead of thinking about the order in which guests will greet you, focus on ensuring that all your guests feel welcomed at the festivities.

If the wedding is being given in your own home, you may not want to play the role of hostess because you prefer the part of bride only on this special day. Look at it this way—a bride receives homage; a hostess performs duties. That's why Jill asked a friend to play hostess at her reception, a cocktail party following the ceremony at her large colonial home.

"There were several reasons why I picked Lynette for the

part," explained Jill. "First of all, because I've known her for so many years, she knew just about everyone I knew, from the guests coming from my hometown, which she's visited with me, to my colleagues at the job I've had less than a year, whom she met at my Christmas party. Beside that, Lynette's a natural hostess. Maybe it's her Southern background, which makes her so gregarious and gracious," Jill reflected. "Whatever it is, it worked like a charm at my reception."

It was Lynette who cheerfully took on the meet-and-greet functions, then made certain everyone was mixing and mingling, deftly pulling bashful guests into cozy conversational circles, striking up conversations with those on the sidelines till she could maneuver them into a suitable cluster. That way Jill could be the radiant bride, enfolded by family and friends in warm embraces. She was the adored object of her groom's lavish attentions without having to worry that no one was talking to Gramps or that her secretary was hovering on the edge of several conversations without being drawn into any.

Just as the bride need not be hostess at her own reception, the person at whose home a reception is being held need not automatically assume the role. "My very good friend, Gail, gave me the wedding reception in her large duplex apartment," Coral recalled. The bride and groom provided a caterer who served a sumptuous buffet supper and a full bar. "But we knew we'd need somebody other than Gail to kind of pull things together, to make introductions and start conversations because a lot of the guests didn't know one another." While Gail had a fabulous apartment and a generous nature, she was not one of those women who took easily to the role of hostess. Coral's mother, however, was exactly that sort and was thrilled when her daughter asked her to do the hostessing honors.

"She performed them beautifully, just as I knew she would," Coral said proudly. "I was glad to be able to give my mother a definite function at my wedding. She had been so involved in planning my first one and had been feeling left out of this one, although she didn't say so."

You may be feeling some uneasy stirrings vaguely resembling an emotion called guilt as you read these words. Don't. Or at least if you do, take it as going with the territory of being a second-time bride. Your first wedding was probably planned primarily by your mother. Since this one is yours, your mother may very well be feeling left out. If there's some special function for your mother to perform at your second nuptials, like hostessing, baking the cake, or any other arrangements which she can oversee, by all means ask her to give you a hand.

One area in which you will definitely need help if you have small children is getting someone to keep an eye on them. Tact is called for here. Your new mother-in-law might be flattered by the request that she do so, especially if she's eager to be a grandmother, or she might be insulted that you're singling her out to do a chore. The point is to know of whom you are asking what, and the meaning that has to them before barging in with unwelcomed requests. The childcare position must be filled, though, even if it means hiring a babysitter. As a mother, you know all too well that if several adults are vaguely in charge of childcare, the mother ends up being specifically so. You can't be radiant bride and responsible mom all at once, so make sure someone is there to take care of small children.

If you're having a sit-down meal, be it casual brunch or black-tie dinner, the question of an MC arises. Some catering establishments or hotels provide such hardy souls along with the linen and place settings. However, a hired stranger performing what should be so personal a function may go against the grain of the individuality and authenticity you want for your second wedding. If one of your guests has a personality suited to such a role ask him—or her—to perform it. One couple whose close friend is an aspiring stand-up comic asked her to take charge of the after-dinner comments.

"Casey likes to think of herself as a contemporary female

reincarnation of Lenny Bruce," the bride said with a mischievous smile, "so, of course, we had to warn her to tone down her routine, which obligingly she did, keeping just to the conservative side of outrageous."

Fit the function to the personality performing it and you can't go wrong. If the best man is the most loyal pal a groom ever had but he's terrified of speaking in public, don't force him to make the toast just because tradition dictates he be the first to raise his glass in tribute to the newlyweds. Maybe you have an aunt with a magnetic presence and a resonant voice, or a great uncle with a gift of blarney that can turn a routine toast into pure poetry. Don't hesitate calling on these talents to enhance the reception. And speaking of toasts, there's no reason the bride and groom can't raise their glasses and their voices in words of praise to each other.

"Jerry and I had a formal marriage ceremony in the minister's study," said Myrna, who married for the second time a year ago. "But we still had the urge to convey our deep love, our sense of commitment in public." She and Jerry did just that in the toasts they made to each other at the wedding dinner. Other couples have called upon their friends and their children to say a few words, but never without asking that person beforehand. One bride was thrilled when her eight-year-old daughter offered to recite a poem she had written for her mother and new stepfather. Another couple who between them have five teenage children let the kids put on a skit for after-dinner entertainment at the wedding.

"They wrote it themselves. It was all about how we met and the various disasters of our early dating days. It was tasteful, touching, and amusing all at once," the proud father fondly recalled. When it comes to the program of performances at a wedding reception, call on those you care about to do what they do best. The results will be more delightful than you can imagine.

Another wedding tradition you'll want to take a long look at is dancing. Some couples decide against it because of contingencies of space or because it creates a more formal atmosphere than they wish. One considerate bride decided against ballroom dancing for another reason:

"A lot of my friends were coming without escorts and very few of my husband's were," Rosemary explained. "The last thing I wanted was for any of my single women friends to feel like wallflowers," Rosemary said. "But we did have plenty of dancing. Since my background is Irish and my husband is Israeli, there were plenty of group folk dances we could do which don't call for partners."

At the other extreme was the couple still in their twenties who had a rock band at their reception. "With the kind of nontouch dancing our friends do, it doesn't matter if a person dances alone, or joins a twosome and no one thinks anything of it if two women dance together. An uneven ratio of females to males isn't a problem for anyone who wants to get out there and dance," explained the groom.

Three other wedding traditions which you may want to retain, eliminate, or enhance to suit your tastes are the cutting of the wedding cake, tossing the bridal bouquet, and throwing rice at the departing newlyweds.

You'll probably want to cut the first slice of wedding cake even if it's not the many-tiered creation of a first wedding. Feeding a piece to the groom is optional. Do it if you feel good doing so, don't if it makes you feel foolish. One couple made the cake cutting into a new kind of ritual. The bride cut a slice of the single-tiered cake, put a piece in the groom's mouth, and then fed pieces to each of his three children, after which he did the same with her son and her daughter.

"It made for a cozy family feeling," the bride noted.

When it comes to tossing the bridal bouquet, you can again keep or discard the tradition as you see fit. One bride who didn't carry a bouquet impulsively tossed her corsage to the cluster of her female friends standing at the bottom of the stairs in her house as she went up to change. Other second-time brides who have carried bouquets have chosen not to toss them.

"It just didn't feel right to me," said one woman in her forties. "Most of my friends are married, and for those who aren't, somehow I didn't think they would enjoy reaching out to catch a bouquet." Another bride simply handed her bouquet to a friend who had recently become engaged. Other brides toss them to whoever wants to catch. To toss the bouquet or not is up to you. It's also something you can decide at the last moment. If you have opted to carry a cluster of long-stemmed flowers rather than a bouquet, you could give out the flowers to your female friends and relatives.

Whether or not you and your new husband are going to dash off to a waiting car under a shower of rice, in some cases mixed with rose petals, will probably not be a spur-of-the-moment decision. Since it's usually done as a surprise, it is likely to be an affectionate gesture on the part of your wedding guests. If you are leaving the wedding while your guests are still around, there is a good chance you will be showered with rice. If you want to have rice thrown, make sure someone in the wedding party knows it and will arrange to hand it out to the guests as you depart.

Deciding how to end your wedding is another decision you and your groom will have to make. You may opt for the grand exit, or choose to stay after your guests have left. If the wedding reception has been a brunch given in your home and you still have hours before the departure of your honeymoon flight, you can spend those hours at home with your new husband and your children. In that case, you'll be saying goodbye to your guests as they go. Perhaps there are a few particularly close friends and family members you can invite to linger over another cup of coffee and an extra slice of wedding cake. This can be a cozy time to help the kids make the transition from wedding day to the realities of a new family life, which may well begin with your departure for the honeymoon.

If your next-door neighbor drives you to the airport, your

children and parents could throw handfuls of rice at the departing car. Or maybe they'll come with you to the airport and toss a few symbolic grains as you go through security. Expect happy surprises and welcome gestures of warmth and joy. Your new marriage will be rich in both of them.

CHAPTER NINETEEN

Après-nuptial Arrangements

In the movies, the newlyweds drive off amid a shower of rice without a thought to what they're leaving behind. But as you've probably noticed by now, reel life is a far cry from real life. Only if you make some practical arrangements beforehand can you then go off into the sunset with a free mind.

Entertaining out-of-town guests could be one of your responsibilities now. In a first-time wedding, the mother of the bride usually takes on this obligation. She may give them supper following an afternoon wedding, or in the case of an evening wedding, perhaps she will put some of them up for the night and serve them a brunch the next day. But in a second wedding, these arrangements are usually left up to you. Since you may well be in transition between apartments, houses, etc., you could offer out-of-town friends accommodations at one of these homes. If this is not possible, make sure that your guests have taken care of their own accommodations.

Another thing to plan for is just where you will spend your wedding night. Even if you've postponed the honeymoon for several weeks or even a few months, the two of you will want at least one night away before going back home. Most couples who put off the honeymoon try for at least a few days alone at some quiet inn, or even a night in a glamorous hotel. Some hotels offer one night's complimentary stay to couples who have had their wedding reception there. This could serve either as your mini-honeymoon or a lovely place to spend the night before leaving on your wedding trip.

Whatever your own post-wedding plans, if there are children involved, you'll want to make certain that careful arrangements have been made for them in your absence. If they are staying with friends over the one night you'll be away, make sure they know the exact arrangements for their care. When you are dealing with your new husband's children, some tricky problems can crop up if you're not prepared for them.

"Glenn and I were going away for the weekend right after the wedding because we had postponed the honeymoon till the following month," said Cynthia, the mother of three. "The wedding took place at the country club near my home, where Glenn was already living. After the reception, my parents drove my kids and Glenn's there to spend the weekend together. It seemed like a good idea at the time, since Glenn's children live with their mother over a two-hour drive from us. But it turned into a disaster," Cynthia regretfully reported. "Although we thought both sets of kids accepted the marriage, angry quarrels erupted between my children and Glenn's, which my parents had difficulty handling. Glenn's kids finally phoned their mother and asked her to come and get them, although they knew their father was planning to drive them home on his return. Since there was already a lot of resentment on Glenn's ex-wife's part, her having to make this unexpected trip only added fuel to the fire of her grievances and marred the period immediately following the wedding."

Cynthia's unfortunate tale should sound a clear warning that if you're dealing with a resentful ex-wife, it would behoove you to give some thought as to how your new stepchildren are going to get home after you and their father have floated off on your happy cloud. If there are any wedding guests who live near your stepchildren, arrange beforehand to have them taken home by these guests. If not, their father should arrange for relatives or close friends whom they already know well to take the children back to their mother.

It is very important that in the last-minute rush which all weddings entail, neither your children nor his feel ignored, abandoned, or neglected when the newlyweds go off together. If you are leaving your children at home with your mother, another relative, a close friend, or a reliable housekeeper while you are on your honeymoon, make sure that person is aware of all the specifics of the kids' schedules. You don't want your son to miss his Little League practice because Mother, off on her honeymoon, forgot to make the arrangements to have him driven there on Thursday afternoon. Nor do you want to wake up in Maui struck with something you forgot to tell your mother about calling the plumber. So take time in the frenetic pre-wedding days to make plans for what should go on in your house in your post-wedding absence.

Another pitfall to avoid is putting your children in strange surroundings while you're away. If you and your husband are in the process of moving into a new home you haven't actually lived in yet, it's a mistake to have the children stay there while you are on your honeymoon, even if they are with grandparents or other people to whom they are very close.

Avoid doing anything to make your children feel disoriented during this period of transitions. It has been difficult for them, no matter how accepting they are of your remarriage. If it is feasible for your children to stay with their father or with close friends rather than in a house they haven't lived in before, there would be far less disruption for them. In fact, a major move coming right on the heels of the wedding is reason enough to seriously consider postponing the honeymoon till you're all settled in the new home.

Even if you are staying in the same home and the man you're marrying has been living there with you and your children for some time, you should be aware that the very fact of the wedding may bring out hidden insecurities in your kids. This is why you should plan to put aside extra time to spend with your children when you return from your honeymoon. Remember that this is as much a period of adjustment for them as it is for you. Fears and fantasies of being excluded from this new married life may loom larger in your children than you realize.

The more plans you make for your children during your honeymoon, the easier a period it will be for them. Arrange for them to be taken out for a meal, go on an outing, or stay overnight with grandparents, aunts and uncles, or friends of yours with whom they are particularly close. Before you leave, tell the children all the plans you've made. If you have a family bulletin board in the kitchen, post notices there. Before you go away, make sure the children know that you are thinking of them and that you care how their time is spent in your absence. Check school schedules and extracurricular activities to make sure that if there is any event parents are expected to attend while you are away, someone is designated to go in your place.

In the throes of the (often irrational) guilt you may be feeling about leaving your children, especially younger ones, to go on your honeymoon, you may make promises you won't want to keep. If you're going to be rafting on the Columbia River, you obviously can't commit yourself to calling every night. But even if you're at a luxury hotel, you may feel pressured about returning from a romantic excursion in time to make that nightly call. Of course, you will be making some calls but it is wise not to corner yourself into saying exactly when and how often you will call. Also, don't promise presents that may not be easy to find or to carry.

Keep your promises about what you will do for your children while on your honeymoon as limited as possible. Otherwise, you may feel conflicts during the time spent with your brand-new husband. Instead, tell your children about the fun things you plan to do with them on your return. However, if you already know that you will return from your honeymoon to find an overflowing desk at the office, a mountain of thank-you notes to write, and possibly a new home to move into and furnish, go easy on promises to the kids about immediate mini-vacations. The last thing you want to do at this time when they are so vulnerable is to raise expectations you won't be able to meet.

Even if you have postponed your honeymoon, the post-nuptial period may still feel strange for your children—and for you. You and your new husband might be in a romantic mood in which you crave more privacy than usual while your children, anxious about the changes in your life, may make more demands for your attention than usual. If your new husband has moved into your home immediately following the wedding, his children may want to see him at times other than scheduled visits. If your husband's ex-wife has not remarried, this can be a trying time for her and she may suddenly find problems which only he can take care of. There's no way you can avoid all the tensions created by the reality of your marriage, but it helps to be prepared for them.

If you've spent feverish weeks planning the wedding and the honeymoon has been postponed, you may be in for a bit of a letdown as life goes from the sublime to the routine. While it's hard to avoid some feelings of depression, they won't be as acute if they are anticipated. Whether the honeymoon is postponed or not, the moment eventually comes when you have to live up to those promises in your thank-you notes about so-and-so coming to dinner to see how lovely their silver candlesticks look on your table.

Handle the post-nuptial depression by, first of all, not denying its existence. Don't fear that a disillusion with your new marriage has set in. You're simply adjusting to normal life after the romantic raptures of the past months. But don't settle too solidly into the routine. Now is the time to keep the romantic fires fanned. True, they won't always burn as brightly as they did during the days just before your marriage, but work on keeping a warm glow going which will sustain and inspire in the years ahead.

If the preceding paragraphs have caught you up short in the middle of your wedding plans with the reminder that happily ever after is only in fairy tales, take heart. One of the advantages of having been married before is that unrealistic expectations are tempered by the teachings of experience. Since you don't expect a storybook ending, you won't be disappointed that there isn't one. What you will be is amply prepared for the ups and downs in your new married life. And with such a seasoned attitude, the prospects for keeping the feelings of love strong during the post-nuptial adjustment period and beyond are truly optimistic.

CHAPTER TWENTY

Happy Honeymoon

The wedding trip should crown your nuptials with a respite from cares and a chance to discover even more of each other than you have already learned. Now that your second wedding has proved to be all you've ever wished for, just follow these easy directions to your dream honeymoon.

Don't Delay Too Long

In every second bride's bill of rights, a *real* honeymoon should rank high. The only reason you should postpone that glorious experience is if you're caught in too much of a time crunch about wedding plans and/or the season in which you want to get married and the one in which you want to take your wedding trip don't coincide. In this case, a weekend, preferably a long one, or at the very least one night, should be spent by the two of you alone and away from home. If you do choose to postpone the honeymoon, don't do so for more than a few months and put aside the time on which you will be taking it *before* the wedding.

Unless you set a specific date for the trip, you are liable to end up putting it off for many, many months, even years. Once indefinitely postponed, the honeymoon can recede from your horizon like an elusive dream upon waking. You may find yourself planning your wedding trip several times, but having it turned into a harried family vacation with two sets of stepkids. Also, if the trip you finally take is too far removed in time from the nuptial period, it will not be a genuine honeymoon.

A honeymoon can be even more crucial in getting a second marriage off to the right start than a first. The early months of a first marriage are known as the honeymoon period for good reason. The young couple with no child-rearing responsibilities can turn their bedroom into a nightly honeymoon suite, their Sunday morning strolls into a grand tour, and afternoons at the nearest beach into a trip to a tropical paradise. Not so the second wife who is also a career woman, mother, and (very likely) stepmother to a few demanding weekend guests. That's why it is even more important for you to have a honeymoon this time around. A *real* honeymoon does not mean a few weekends wrested from family obligations. It means at least one week off by yourselves in a place you both ardently want to be. And that week should come, if not immediately following the marriage, no more than six months later, though the sooner the better to retain the nuptial aura.

No Repeat Performance Permitted

In Neil Simon's romantic comedy *Act II*, a still-grieving widower takes his eager bride on a honeymoon to the Caribbean hotel which was the favorite vacation spot of him and his deceased wife. This bizarre choice made sense in terms of the script simply because it served to illustrate that the new husband had not yet emotionally accepted his first wife's death and was trying to keep her alive in this problematic second marriage. It came as no surprise to anyone in the audience when the honeymoon turned into a disaster. Remember: A honeymoon should be the first step on the path of your new life together—*not* a trip down memory lane.

Do not, repeat, do not return to the scene of happy times with an ex or deceased spouse of either the bride or groom. You might also want to beware of a more subtle variation on this dangerous theme. "When Dick suggested a honeymoon in Paris, I was thrilled," said Karen, a personnel director for a Midwestern corporation. Karen had never been to Europe, and the honeymoon of her first, short-lived marriage had been in the Great Lakes. Karen was eager to see something of the world with her widely traveled second husband, and she knew that Dick and his first wife had honeymooned in Mexico, so Paris sounded perfectly safe from painful memories.

Although Karen knew that Dick and Julie had each separately lived in Paris for a short period of their lives, she didn't realize the emotional significance of that city in the earlier marriage. In fact, she knew little of her husband's relationship with his first wife except that her leaving him for another man had been a devastating experience.

"Even though he and Julie had never been there at the same time, Paris, it turned out, played a big part in their fantasies," Karen explained. "It seems they were always talking about going back there together. As Dick was showing me all those famous, fabulous sights and taking me to his favorite out-of-the-way places, I sensed he was thinking of what might have been there for him and Julie."

Karen's second marriage survived the painful memories the honeymoon evoked in her husband. But it took considerable counseling for the couple to work out their problems. They had to deal with both Dick's unresolved feelings for his first wife and with Karen's anger about the emotional intrusion of her predecessor into the honeymoon. The way for you to avoid a similar situation is to make certain beforehand that the scene of your second honeymoon has no past emotional associations, however indirect, for either you or your new husband.

Compatibility Is Your Key to Honeymoon Happiness

If he's always talking about teaching you how to ski or you want to introduce him to scuba diving, the honeymoon is *not* the time to try something so new to one of you. Suppose you turn out to have a fear of heights once on the slopes, or he turns out to have a touch of claustrophobia in his underwater mask? The discovery of such disturbing disparities in your tastes can mar the emotional ambience which makes for a blissful honeymoon. Even if you take to skiing or he to scuba diving, you may find one of you in the beginners' classes and the other in the advanced. Hardly an exercise in the togetherness a honeymoon is meant to be!

If the honeymoon is to be built around a sport, make sure it is one you both enjoy, and in which you are somewhat equally matched. If you both love horseback riding and are approximately at the same level of proficiency in the saddle but haven't had the time to pursue this pleasure together, a dude ranch might make a marvelous honeymoon. If, on the other hand, neither of you has ever skied before, don't go to an alpine winter resort expecting to both fall in love with the sport because only one of you may do so, which is hardly a situation made for getting a new marriage off to a compatible start.

Avoid extremes of experience unless you can equally share them. If he's got a bit of the beach bum in him and you're into art museums, the Caribbean may not be for you, but neither is Europe in winter. You might try accommodating both tastes by dividing a ten-day winter trip, with five days in San Francisco and the other five on the Baja Peninsula. In warmer weather, you could split a week in New England between Boston and the beaches of Cape Cod. Or if your time and money permits, you could have a week in Rome and/or Florence, maybe the last week of May when it's summer in Northern Italy, followed by a week of fun in the sun on the Italian Riviera.

Even if neither of you has been to Europe before, don't do one of those whirlwind tours of eight countries in fourteen days unless you're both avid sightseers with a taste for life in the fast lane. Be imaginative in mixing and matching your separate preferences to make for combined pleasure. If he thrives on boating excursions and you crave exotic sights rife with legend and history, a cruise around the Greek isles could be just the thing for the two of you. If he loves pub crawling and you get a thrill from theatergoing, a week in London could merge your two interests with happy results all around.

Match the Honeymoon to Your Nuptial Mood

Just as different couples have different desires and needs to meet when it comes to planning a wedding, so too with the honeymoon. Stay attuned to each other's feelings, talk through your expectations for the wedding trip thoroughly, taking both financial and emotional factors into consideration. If you're frazzled from wintry weeks of wedding preparations and want to beachcomb from sunrise to sunset, a trip to a tropical island might be the tonic to eradicate all the accumulated tensions. If your finances are strained, if you love the Caribbean and don't mind the heat, an off-season honeymoon to the island of your choice following a summer wedding can cut expenses to about half of what they'd be in the midwinter high season. Should you be in the mood to soak in a foreign culture but don't want to spend the money to go abroad, there's always New Orleans or Quebec for a French atmosphere.

What is an escape for some couples is too much like home

for others. The city subway rider might find it romantic to rent a car and take off for the nearest mountains or seashore, sharing the driving with her new husband. But for the suburban carpooling mom, a get-away-from-it-all trip might mean not having to operate a motor vehicle the whole time. If you and the man you just married both do a lot of traveling for business but don't have enough privacy at home because of the children from both marriages, just being alone together in a remote spot might be your idea of paradise. But for two people whose work never takes them out of the office and who have plenty of time to be alone together evenings and weekends, a trip taking in a wide variety of locations could be perfect.

Whatever your circumstances, if you gauge your mood accurately and then plan your honeymoon to suit it, you can't go wrong.

Tried and True

Just because it's your second honeymoon, there's no need to blaze new paths in travel history. If offbeat vacations aren't your thing, go to your travel agent and find out what looks enjoyable and affordable in the way of island cruises, Bermuda cottages, or Mexican packaged tours. But find a sufficiently sympathetic travel agent to appreciate the fact that this *is* your honeymoon and not simply another vacation. You need to plan your trip with someone who understands how important it is that there be no unsuspected flaws to disrupt your idyll.

You don't want be be in a bungalow colony with college-age newlyweds if you're in your forties, nor do you want a cruise made up almost entirely of retirees if you're in your thirties. You don't want a resort catering to the swinging singles crowd as you take your first steps into matrimonial waters. A good travel agent will be on the alert for just such jarring contrasts and steer you clear of them. Travel agents are a breed which run the range from those with a high degree of sensitivity to a client's preferences to others whose indifference never deserts them. If neither of you has a travel agent of your own, it's best to get the name of one from a friend or colleague whose opinion you can trust. If you do go to a travel agent who has no track record with anyone you know and your instincts say this person is not taking the time and interest you want from the planner of your honeymoon, find another agent.

Exotic Experiences

Many couples who enter a second marriage have done a lot of traveling on their own and have already taken several trips together. They want to make their honeymoon a truly unique trip but can't think their way past European capitals, Mexican mountains, or Hawaiian beaches. If you and your new husband fall into this category, here are some creative suggestions which will give you a rare and remarkable honeymoon adventure.

"All a couple needs is ten days to two weeks, five to six thousand dollars depending on whether they want deluxe or standard accommodations, and an adventurous spirit and I can plan them a honeymoon which will be sheer magic," promises Frances Wollach, a New York travel agent.

"Romantic, exotic, and delicious" is Wollach's description of Bora Bora in the lush South Pacific paradise of Tahiti. The combination of French sophistication with Polynesian exuberance makes for an unbeatable combination of cultural styles. In a hotel of thatched-roofed rooms overlooking the water, you will find undreamed-of seclusion and serenity in fascinating surroundings.

Another intriguing jaunt deep into the mysteries of the East is a trip to both Bangkok and Bali. The capital of Thailand, Bangkok has been called "the Venice of Asia" because of its elaborate network of canals. You can take a trip on a river boat stopping at floating markets for the most unique shopping experience in the world. A one-day excursion from Bangkok takes you to Chiang Mai, an extraordinarily beautiful city graced with an awe-inspiring Buddhist temple. From these treasures of Thailand, you go on to Indonesia and the incomparable charm of Bali, a densely populated little island known as "the Paradise of the Pacific." Colorful ceremonies and celebrations attest to the omnipresent attractions of the exotic customs which characterize Balinese Hinduism. For exercise, you can swim in either the Indian Ocean or the Flores Sea depending on which side of the island you find yourselves.

Another enticing possibility is a trip which takes you to a South Pacific trio of exotica encompassing Bangkok, the Fiji Islands, and Singapore. Among the many charms of the chain of Melanesian islands collectively called Fiji are the vividly colored flowers; the cosmopolitan culture of South Sea Islanders mingling with Indian, Sikh, Chinese, and European influences; and the magnificent sight of the surf breaking on coral reefs. Then there's Singapore, an island seductive in exotic treasures from the world-famous mosques and temples.

For an equally romantic Asian honeymoon, you can spend two weeks in Northern India and Nepal. From viewing the Taj Mahal by moonlight to the Himalayas towering over Katmandu, you will be enthralled by sights which will never leave your memories. The same is true of an Egyptian honeymoon in which your two weeks include a cruise up the Nile to villages amid Greek and Roman ruins where time stands still. This intriguing excursion is followed by a stay in a Cairo hotel surrounded by pyramids and sphinxes while offering all the modern luxuries, including a swimming pool and intriguingly cosmopolitan ambience. From Cairo you fly to Abu Simbal and the ruins of the temple of Ramses II with its gigantic and haunting carvings.

For the same expenditure of time and money, you can spend two weeks on an African safari, winding up in the Seychelles Islands, tropical jewels in the Indian Ocean. Or perhaps you prefer North Africa and a trip by camel through the Tunesian desert where you will learn how to bathe in sand, and end your trip doing your bathing in a deluxe resort on the Mediterranean Sea. For an alternative North African adventure, spend a dozen days in Morocco, from the rose-pink oasis city of Marrakech to the picturesque seafront town of Agadir.

Should your wanderlust lead you to the wonders of the New World, you can travel through Peru, flying from Lima to Cuzco, the ancient capital of the Incas high in the mountains with its fascinating mixture of Indian and Spanish civilizations. From there you take a train to Machu Picchu, the mountaintop sanctuary of the Inca rulers in times of peril. Another plane ride from Lima takes you to Iquitos, a jungle city from which you can take a day's boat trip down the Amazon. Still another South American adventure is a ten-day trip to Ecuador, dividing your time between a cruise of the Galápagos Islands, where you can follow the course of Darwin's voyage of discovery, and a stay in Quito, a city of magnificent views and famous art treasures, a day's trip from remote mountain villages.

For still another exotic honeymoon, charter a private yacht along with your own crew and cruise the British Virgin Islands or the Grenadines for one week. The cost of this voyage is between forty-five hundred and six thousand dollars, including airfare. Your yacht makes daily stops at different islands where your captain can arrange diving or tennis or any other activity you wish to pursue. Evenings are spent on deck, dining on one of the delicious dishes your cook has prepared, perhaps steamed lobsters, always a specialty on these cruises.

If these intriguing trips entice you but sound too rich for your blood, remember that they amount to no more than six thousand dollars for two, including airfare, inland travel, and all hotel accommodations, which usually include two meals a day. According to a recent article in the *New York Times*, the average wedding in the United States ran about $13,500 in 1987. Perusing the earlier chapters of this book again, you will recall numerous suggestions for making your nuptials less formal, more free-style. Keeping in mind that such second weddings can be far less expensive than elaborate first weddings, you may realize that you do indeed have the funds for a truly exotic honeymoon.

It's an option you should certainly consider. If there's one lesson those with the courage to embark on a second marriage have learned, it is to live fully and expansively. You deserve to have your second wedding and honeymoon be enriching and fulfilling experiences because you have dared to try again. And in that spirit of daring lies your greatest hope for success in this new life you are launching. Bon Voyage.

ABOUT THE AUTHOR

Judith Slawson is a graduate of the University of Michigan and a former English teacher and guidance counselor. She is the author of the acclaimed biography of iconoclastic movie star *Robert Duvall: Hollywood Maverick* (St. Martin's Press, 1985) and the popular novel about a trio of lady lawyers, *Legal Affairs* (Pocket Books, 1988). She is now at work on her second novel.

Ms. Slawson was married for the second time in 1986 in the suburban home of a close friend. She and her husband, a building contractor, happily divide their time between homes in downtown Manhattan and upstate New York.

7794 40 89